# MY 30 YEARS WITH THE CALIFORNIA DEPARTMENT OF CORRECTIONS

# MY 30 YEARS WITH THE CALIFORNIA DEPARTMENT OF CORRECTIONS

## THIRTY YEARS OF INCARCERATION...
## LED TO HIS MIRACULOUS TRANSFORMATION!

*For my friend John.*

*[signature]*

Terrance Dwayne Hunter

Palmetto Publishing Group
Charleston, SC

*My 30 Years with the California Department of Corrections*
Copyright © 2018 by Terrance Hunter
All rights reserved

The content of this publication was edited by the author, Terrance Hunter.

First Edition

Printed in the United States

ISBN-13: 978-1-64111-287-1
ISBN-10: 1-64111-287-5

# TABLE OF CONTENTS

# ACKNOWLEDGMENT

I met my beautiful fiancée, Cynthia Yvonne Baugh, on February 12, 2015. It was my first day as an employee at Home Depot, store #1861, in San Jose, California. We passed each other on aisle #19, and as I glanced back at her, I discovered she was also glancing back at me. Cynthia had been working there for several years. In the process of getting to know her, I told Cynthia I had recently been released from prison, after serving 30 years for a 1985 second degree murder conviction. I also shared certain information concerning my background, and the fact, I was writing a book about my life experiences. Cynthia encouraged me to finish my writing project and informed me she was interested in reading what I had written, thus far.

After an infinite number of conversations, over a nine-month period, we decided to bring in the new year (2016), together. Shortly thereafter, we were dating and spending a great deal of time with each other.

In March of 2016, Cynthia, went to Florida, to visit her parents. When Cynthia returned from her trip, she had a laptop computer that was a gift from her father. To my surprise, she gave me the laptop, and said I could use the computer to write my book. A few days later, she received a printer\scanner\copy machine, that her father had purchased for her. Cynthia also gave me the printer\scanner\copy machine. Just like that, Cynthia provided the desktop publishing equipment, that has enabled me to write this book.

I would like to acknowledge Cynthia for the joy, love, and inspiration she has brought into my life. Cynthia has consistently supported me in every possible manner, and I can always count on her words of encouragement. I was attracted to her personality and spirit, the day we met, and to this day our relationship continues to soar to higher heights. Cynthia, undoubtedly, you are a precious gift from God, and I feel so Blessed to have found someone whom I feel, I cannot live without. My life has become a rich and more meaningful place, with you in it. Baby, I Love You, so much.

I would like to thank my mother, Anna "Kitty" Jones, for bringing me into this world, for giving me the gift of life. I thank you for overcoming the obstacles you have faced in life, and I appreciate the sacrifices you made along the way.

I want to thank my friend, Bruce Hodgin, for seeing something in me that I could not see in myself. I thank him for believing I was someone who was worth befriending, despite the mistakes I have made in life. More importantly, I thank Bruce for the the father-like love and support he has so freely given me.

I would like to thank Connie Hodgin for befriending and being what I consider a second mother. She has been a warm and caring soul, who has been very supportive of me. Thank you for the visits, phone conversations and most importantly, your love.

I would like to acknowledge Grandma Louise, who is no longer physically with us. Though she has passed on and is in a better place, she remains with me in spirit. I want to thank her for offering to be the surrogate grandmother, I never had. It was a turning point in my life when she made this very unexpected gesture of love and kindness.

I want to thank and acknowledge my dear friend, Sebastian Bosco. After reading a letter I had written to his mother (Grandma Louise), he decided he wanted to meet me. Him and I hit it off from the very beginning and established what I consider to be, a brotherly bond. I can recount the in-depth phone conversations and the heart-felt discussions between him and I in the visiting room at the Correctional Training Facility, in Soledad. He is truly a life-long friend.

I want to thank Victoria Bosco for a friendship that I will always value. The very first time I met Victoria, she wanted to know what her and her family could do to help me gain my release from prison. Victoria told me I was a good person and I no longer deserved to be in prison. As she was speaking to me, the wells of her eyes were filled with tears. I will never forget that moment because it demonstrated to me that from the very beginning, she could see I was not the man I used to be. I also would like to thank Victoria, for writing the Forward to my book.

I would to thank my dear friend, Linda McCue, whom I befriended through my participation in the Alternatives to Violence Project. For more than 10 years, Linda and I have worked side-by-side, as non-violence advocates. I have the utmost respect for Linda's commitment to the Alternatives to Violence Project, because I know her efforts come straight from the heart. It is impossible for me to think about how AVP has impacted my life, without also thinking of Linda. I would also like to thank Linda, for writing the forward to my book.

I want to thank all my fellow AVP Facilitators, both inside and outside prison walls, who are too many to mention. I especially want to thank the members of the AVP Santa Cruz/Salinas Valley Council. Individuals such as George Ramos, Mimi Edgar, Alan Edgar, John Devalcourt, Betty Devalcourt, Robin Keeler, Terrill Keeler and Stacey Hughes. All of you have played a role in my transformation from someone who was a violent person, to a man who believes violence is never a solution to conflict. I look forward to working with and interacting with all of you, for many years to come.

I would like to thank my friend, Dr. Michael Nagler, for responding to my initial letter and sending me his publication, "Is There No Other Way? The Search for a Non-Violent Future." In addition to offering to assist me in my efforts to reduce the violence in prison, Michael also became a confidant. I look forward to possibly working with Michael, in the future.

I want to thank my friend, Dr. David Rollo, for writing the Introduction to my book. I have only known David for a very short period. Yet, the very first time we conversed with one another, it was if we had known each other, forever. The conversation was smooth and effortless, and while we come from totally different backgrounds, we could relate to one another.

I want to thank my friend, Hedi Molla for shooting the photo for the cover of my book. Hedi is not only a friend but a fellow Toastmaster, as well. I met Hedi when I attended my first True Talking Toastmasters meeting, and him and every other member, encouraged me to join the club. Hedi has served as Toastmasters International District 101 Photographer.

Finally, I would like to thank my new-found mentor, Johnny B. It is a relationship that began over a cup of coffee. Well, Johnny B. had coffee, while I enjoyed a glass of juice. It is an unlikely encounter between men at the very opposite ends of the spectrum. Yet, Johnny B. is the mentor I wish I had had as a kid. I want to thank Johnny B. for the time we have spent together, and his efforts to encourage me to passionately pursue my goals.

*From left to right: Sebastian & Victoria Bosco, Terrance Hunter,*
*Connie & Bruce Hodgin. (Photo taken in the Correctional Training*
*Facility visiting room, in Soledad, CA.)*

# FOREWORD

## BY: VICTORIA BOSCO

Never in a million years did I ever imagine myself entering a prison to visit and support a man, who had been convicted of 2nd degree murder and was serving a 17 years to life, prison sentence.

However, that was before I ever heard of Terrance Hunter. What started with a friendly postcard, ended with many letters and visits and a life-long friendship of nearly 20 years.

In this book, Terrance chronologically takes you on a journey as he recalls his life experiences that led him onto a path of recklessness, womanizing and eventually, the loss of a life. This is a compelling account of survival in the California prison system, along with self-examination, personal growth, and considerable determination, that eventually leads to his full rehabilitation. Along the way, Terrance reveals his inner most feelings. Including, the discovery of his internal desire to help other prisoners overcome their uncontrollable tendencies, of using violence to offset their unfulfilled sense of well-being, lack of self-esteem and confidence.

His determination to utilize his time in prison to improve himself and others, led to his participation in many anger management programs and self-help groups, in which he excelled, with flying colors. Terrance has accomplished what he set out to do and beyond. During his period of confinement, he earned a college degree, an A+ Computer Service Technician certification, and several other certificates of accomplishment. Terrance also is a leader in the Toastmasters International Organization and the Alternatives to Violence Project International Organization.

The road takes a turn when Terrance is finally released from prison and able to apply everything he has learned, toward building a successful life on the outside. His story is an awe-inspiring account of accomplishments, that led to his ability to resolve conflicts, in non-violent manners. Furthermore, Terrance has utilized his Toastmasters International platform, to help spread the word of the benefits associated with rehabilitation, that can be reached through determination and self-examination.

Through the wonderful friendship that we have developed, Terrance has opened my eyes to the realization that everyone deserves a chance to turn their life around and become an asset to our society. I am so thankful for our relationship and the fact that I sent him, that very first postcard...

Victoria Bosco

# FOREWORD

## BY: LINDA MCCUE

When I first met Terrance Hunter, he struck me as a wise, gentle, thoughtful man. It was my first time in prison and I did not know what to expect. Would the inmates be big, surly scary guys? Would I be in danger? I was helping to bring the Alternatives to Violence Project to Soledad prison and Terrance, and two other inmates, were trained facilitators who worked with us in the first workshops. What I found were three intelligent, thoughtful, amiable men who were eager to help in any way they could. The inmate facilitators had been facilitating workshops longer than I had and knew the inside workings of the prison, as well, so they greased the wheels of our initial projects. All three of these facilitators guided me gently through my first few workshops, overcoming my fears and inexperience. We worked together in teams of four or five facilitators to empower inmates to live lives of nonviolence. This is done in an experiential style that empowers people through affirmation, respect for all, community building, cooperation and trust. We cover such topics as nonviolent conflict resolution, non-blaming interpersonal communication and self-esteem.

When I began facilitating with Terrance in 2006, we worked on many teams together and I learned a great deal from him. He always brought a gentle wisdom to our work. Over the years, I got to see him in many different circumstances, some of which would test the patience of anyone. He always remained calm, patient and kind to everyone. After he was paroled, we began facilitating youth AVP workshops together. It was such a joy to work together with young people on the outside after having worked together with inmates for so many years. Terrance brought the same gentle wisdom to the young people that he shared in the prison, but he also injected a joyful, playful manner into the workshops. The young people loved Terrance and were deeply moved by his story.

Terrance's book tells his story from his childhood through his incarceration to his time after prison, when he is working for nonviolence in many ways and through various organizations. He works with young people and adults and with people recently released from prison. He is a shining example of a person who used his time in prison to struggle with and master his own demons and to develop his own considerable potential. He now lives a life of service, grateful to be able to use his gifts to help others.

The world is a better place for Terrance's presence in it and he is eager to share his story. Happy reading and growing.

Linda McCue
Alternatives to Violence Facilitator
AVP Santa Cruz/Salinas Valley Council

# INTRODUCTION

Terrance Hunter was born a poor African American, fathered by an individual he still does not know. Terrance grew up as an angry, bitter and resentful child with a very poor self-image. Typically, most of his confrontations resulted in aggressive or violent behavior. He moved out of his home to live by himself at age 15, experiencing many difficult and dangerous encounters along the way. Unfortunately, one of those difficult encounters involved Terrance taking the life of a close friend, over a situation in which Terrance felt betrayed. This led to Terrance's conviction of second-degree murder with a sentence of 17 years to life in State prison.

During his early years in prison, Terrance continued to suffer from low self-esteem and had great difficulty with anger management. Also, in those early years, Terrance did not consider the consequences that his situation had on others. It was his position that he was the one serving time, taking the punishment and dealing with everything else. The "macho" image he had of himself at the time of his arrest bolstered his belief that he could take care of himself in any hostile environment.

Unfortunately, the anger episodes he had in prison resulted in the denial of parole several times, and his prison term was extended to 30 years. He eventually recognized the need to participate in prison-sponsored programs, and this resulted in Terrance having a life-changing experience. He was be-friended by a man (Bruce Hodgin) who had had a similarly poor relationship with his biological father. After much discussion, the two men bonded. Bruce invited Terrance to be adopted into his immediate family, consisting of a loving wife and children, and later into his extended family of in-laws. The experience of this loving family relationship gradually transformed Terrance from an angry, bitter man to a different kind of person who came to realize that he had never even asked forgiveness for any of his acts of violence ---in fact, he had always felt justified by them.

Soon after, Terrance experienced a strong "Spiritual Awakening" to the presence of God's grace, mercy and blessings. The anger, resentment and darkness within him began to disappear. His viewpoint concerning his incarceration shifted to one of acceptance, and simultaneously from a spiritual and mental perspective, he became totally free.

At this point he embarked on a new journey to participate and facilitate in a variety of self-improvement programs, including *Alternatives to Violence Project*, *SQUIRES*, *Cage Your Rage*, and *Advanced Anger Management*.

Terrance gives credit to the influence of Bruce's family who cared about his wellbeing and showed him love and trust as being the turning point in his life. He cites that this was the key factor in his ability to begin establishing meaningful relationships and friendships and to have the confidence to attend various self-improvement programs. ***He is also convinced that the loving relationship he established with the family played a major role in the way he was able to process, receive and utilize the information conveyed in self-help programs.***

Terrance's life today is about being given the unmerited, undeserved, and unearned gift, of a second chance. For the rest of his life, he has chosen to serve God and strive to be the man that God intended him to be. He hopes to especially help the youth of today so they don't become the prisoners of tomorrow. He encourages fathers to show up and be present in their children's lives. He is an advocate of non-violence and committed to convincing youth and adults that violence is never the solution.

**This true story is a must read for anyone who believes in the miracle of transformation through love and faith.**

F. David Rollo M.D., PhD.
Professor Diagnostic Imaging (Ret)
Vanderbilt University Medical Center

# CHAPTER 1

## MY CHILDHOOD

## DESTINATION CALIFORNIA

My name is Terrance Hunter, and I was born in Charleston, West Virginia, on August 15, in 1959. There was nothing extraordinary about my childhood. I was born in a Baptist home and my mother, siblings and I attended church, at least three times per week. I attended school regularly, followed my mother's instructions, and was an overall, well-behaved child.

As a young boy, I was kind-hearted and cared about the welfare of others. In my neighborhood, I mowed lawns in the summer and shoveled snow during the winter. I can remember how I would have my mower or shovel in hand and I would simply mow a lawn that needed to be mowed or cleared a side walk covered with snow. Sometimes men and women would come out to thank and give me a quarter or fifty cents for my efforts. Other times, they would come out to thank and advise me, they were unable to compensate me for my services. I would let them know it is OK and I did not expect them to pay me anything. I received satisfaction from doing good deeds.

On weekends, I went to local supermarkets and helped women, by carrying groceries to their cars. They would always financially reward me for my assistance. Though I would purchase potato chips, candy, and other snacks with money I earned, I also purchased loaves of bread, sticks of butter or something else that was getting low, in our cupboards or refrigerator. Whenever I purchased food items for our family, I felt like I was contributing to the household and helping my mother.

For two years, during the summer I helped clean local parks and creeks. The program was called MANPOWER, and it afforded under-age kids an opportunity to perform community service activities and earn a little money in the process. At the age of 12, I obtained my first paper route and steady flow of income. The money I earned as a paper boy enabled me to relieve my mother of the obligation of purchasing my school clothes. That would mark my first sense of independence. Buying my own clothes was a very liberating and gratifying experience.

Until the age of twelve, I was raised by my mother. I never met and still do not know my biological father. I can remember how much it hurt me when I was a kid that my father did not want to be a part of my life. He is responsible for bringing me into the world but did not assume any of his parental responsibilities. The hurt from not knowing my father or what type of person he was, made me angry, bitter and resentful. I felt cheated because I only had one parent, while so many other kids had two.

As I got older, I convinced myself, through self-talk, my father's absence did not matter. I suppressed and internalized my true feelings because I did not know how to express them. Furthermore, I did not feel comfortable discussing them with anyone. My stepfather came into my life when I was twelve years old. By then I had decided I no longer needed a father, so I rejected him. I did not see him as a replacement for my father, even though he was a good man and an ideal male role model. To my regret, I did not put forth an effort to establish a father son relationship with him.

In addition to having low self-esteem because I never knew my father, there were other issues that caused me to develop a low sense of self-worth. As I stated earlier, my mother single-handedly raised me, so there were times in which she received welfare assistance. Quite often my mother sent me to the grocery store and I purchased food with food stamps. I can recall the shame I felt when I would pull food stamps out my pocket to pay the cashier. I felt everyone was looking at me and judging me for being poor.

Regarding my self-image, I am an African American who was born in 1959. When I attended grade school, the only time my text books mentioned people of African descent, was in relation to slavery. I never learned anything concerning the positive contributions that people of African descent, have made to this country or the world in general. It was as if slavery represented the beginning of my history. So, I did not feel good about being poor and a member of a race of people who were viewed as former slaves. From my perspective, I was without a single reason to feel proud or think highly of myself, when I was a kid.

However, that would change when I was about 13 years old because I began playing baseball at the local ballpark. The name of my first baseball team was, "The Engineers", and our uniforms resembled the pinstriped uniforms worn by the New York Yankees. I was a pitcher, and I played first base and center field. I was a pretty good player and frequently my skills enabled my team to win games. My coaches, team-mates and their families, constantly showered me with compliments regarding my performance. I felt like I was a part of a very large family and this family valued and appreciated me. Though my parents never came to my practices or games, my coaches and my team-mate's parents took care of me when I was at the park. Someone always bought me refreshments and offered me a ride home after practices and games. I felt special when I was playing baseball. During this time in my life I felt good about myself. In addition to playing baseball, I also played basketball for Woodrow Wilson, my Junior High School. I played the strong forward position.

Unfortunately, one day my stepfather forced me to quit playing sports because I had to babysit my younger brothers and sister. My mother's work hours changed from day shift to swing shift hours. Whereas, my mother previously was home shortly after 3:00, she now would be working until 11:00 pm. It was summer time, and I had a summer job working at my mother's place of employment. I worked at a hospital and I delivered linen to every floor in the facility. My work hours were from 6:00 am to 3:00 pm. After work I would go to base-ball practice/games. So instead of going to baseball practices/games after work, I now was required to come directly home, to care for my younger siblings.

I vividly remember the day I went to the ballpark to turn in my uniform and inform my coaches and teammates, I was quitting the team. This made me angry because I was being forced to stop do-ing something I enjoyed, and I did not believe my siblings were my responsibility. Today, I have a better understanding of why I was so upset. It was not simply a matter of quitting the team but losing the relationships/friendships I had formed with my team mates, my team mate's families and my coaches. I felt special when I went to the ball park because I received acknowledgement at the ball park that I did not receive at home. Furthermore, my team relied upon my pitching, fielding and batting skills, so I felt guilty about quitting the team and deserting them.

My anger caused me to move away from home, abandoning my family when they needed me. I was a couple months away from my 16th birthday. That would prove to be one of the worst decisions I have ever made and the beginning of countless poor decisions.

Initially, when I left home, I rented a room on the top floor of the YMCA, where I played sports for many years. As someone who went to the YMCA on a regular basis, I knew men rented rooms at the top of the building. The night I left home, I walked to the "Y" (YMCA) and requested a room. The lady at the desk looked at me and said, "Son, how old are you?" I told her I was 15 years old. She glanced at me in a side-way manner and said she did not believe she could rent a room to someone my age. The lady went on to say the manager was on vacation, so she would rent me a room and let him make the final decision. When Albert, the manager returned from his vacation, I explained my situation and informed him I was employed. Albert told me he did not care about my age, so long as I can pay my weekly bill.

The following day after I left home, my mother came to work and attempted to talk to me, but I ignored her. She started crying and it bothered me that I was the cause of the tears that were trickling down her face. However, as much as it bothered me that my mother was crying, my anger apparently trumped her pain, because I refused to communicate with her. The next day my mother made another attempt to speak with me and I resorted to the same tactic of ignoring her. At a certain point, I gave in and let her know how I felt about the entire situation. My mother inquired about my living arrangements and I advised her I was living at the top of the YMCA. She responded, "The YMCA? That is no place for a young boy to live." Mom told me to find an apartment and she would co-sign for me. I located an apartment a block or so away from my high school and it was approximately four or five blocks from my place of employment. During my 10th, 11th and 12th grades in school, I attended school in the morning, worked part time after school and worked full time on weekends. This arrangement permitted me to graduate with my class. Remaining in school and graduating from High School was probably the best decision I ever made, after leaving home.

The building in which I resided, was known as, the Cavalier Apartments. There were all sorts of men and women residing within this building. Some were elderly, most of them were probably in their 30's or 40's. Of course, I was the youngest person living there. Other than I, there was only one other person of African descent, living there. His name was Charles, and he had recently separated from his wife. Charles was probably in his late 30's or early 40's. He was amazed and impressed with the fact, I had my own place at the age of 15. Charles and I hit it off from the beginning, and he became someone in which I "hung-out" with. It did not appear as though he was disturbed or unhappy about the separation from his wife. I say this, because female visitors were in his apartment, on a regular basis. Quite often Charles introduced me to his female visitors because I was either there when they arrived or came by when they were already there. I severed my ties with childhood friends and began keeping company with "grown-ups".

At the age of 16, I was tall for my age and had a mustache. Furthermore, I did not dress like someone my age. Instead of wearing jeans and casual clothing, I preferred dress slacks/shirts and suits. As a teen, I went to night clubs and never was carded.

In my interactions with people, they always assumed I was older than my actual age, and I did everything I could to validate their supposition. As a young man who had my own place and a vehicle, I no longer dated girls my age. I began dating older women (18 years old to early 20' s) who did not care about my age.

At the age of 19, I enlisted in the U.S. Air Force. I did not mention my enlistment to anyone in my family until the day of my departure, for Basic Training. On the day I was to board the plane, I called my mother and oldest sister, Cheryl, and requested they come to my apartment. When they arrived, I told them I joined the Air Force and was leaving for Basic Training, in a matter of hours. I gave my mother the keys to my apartment and told her and my sister they can have my furnishings. Of course, they were shocked to learn I had joined the military and had not mentioned it to them or anyone else. My mother and sister accompanied me to the airport, to see me off. At the airport we discovered a Caucasian girl, my age, had also joined the Air Force, and her and I were on the same flight. As it turned out, this would be the first flight taken by her and I. Her family was very concerned about her safety because it would be her first time away from home. Her mother and father asked me if I would look after their daughter, and I agreed to do so. During the take-off portion of the flight, I remember holding her hand because she was frightened. In Basic Training, we coincidently landed in the same squadron.

My six weeks of basic training took place at Lackland Air Force Base, in San Antonio, Texas. Following my completion of basic training, I reported to Keesler Air Force Base, in Biloxi, Mississippi, for technical training that would take several months to complete. Within a couple days of my arrival, the non-commission officer in charge of my squadron issued me a rope that I wore over the left shoulder of my uniform. The rope signified that I was the leader of my squadron and it was my duty to assemble my squadron in formation each morning to march them to school and assemble them after school, for the returning march to our barracks. In addition to marching my squadron to and from school, my responsibilities also included assigning them cleaning detail duties. In recognition of the leadership qualities my superiors believed I possessed, they entrusted and placed me in a leadership position.

Upon completion of my training at Keesler Air Force Base, I reported to my requested assignment, at Travis Air Force Base, in California. Travis Air Force Base is a Military Airlift Command (MAC) base and I was assigned to the 60th Air Base Group. Arriving at Travis AFB was great. The weather was beautiful, and the West Coast was a totally different scene. Upon my arrival at Travis AFB, I was an Airman First

Class. My initial assignment was at the base's PFO (Postal Finance Office) installation. My primary duties included accounting related tasks to make certain the numbers reflecting our inventory and money in the safe were accurate. According to my job description, I was a finance clerk. Though I was an Airman First Class, I was occupying a position designated for a Technical Sargent and above.

As far as my daily routine and past time activities, I played baseball, basketball and football during my leisure time. I also lifted weights and engaged in other forms of exercise. I spent a great deal of my time "club hopping" in the Bay Area, on weekends. I traveled up to 100 miles to go to certain hot spots. My primary stomping grounds" were Emeryville, Oakland, San Mateo, San Francisco, Walnut Creek and Sacramento. I enjoyed the night life.

My second assignment in the military was an administration position. As an Administrative/Documentation Specialist, my primary responsibilities were maintaining and updating Regulations. I would remain in this position, until honorably discharging from the Air Force.

Upon discharging from the Air Force, I moved in with a friend and his girlfriend. Him and I played sports and lifted weights at the gym on Travis AFB. He worked for Orrick, Herrington & Sutcliffe, an international law firm in San Francisco, California, located in the Transamerica Pyramid building. At the time, Transamerica Mortgage had an opening in the security department. My friend put in a good word for me and following my interview with the head of security, I was hired immediately. Within a few days of my discharge from the Air Force, I was working for Transamerica Mortgages Security unit.

Upon discharging from the military, going to night clubs was something in which I did, frequently. My primary reason for frequenting nightclubs, stemmed from my enjoyment of dancing. There were a few clubs appealed to me. I was partial to the atmosphere at the Palladium and the Cross Roads, in San Francisco, Wine & Roses, and Lucky

Lions, in Oakland, and my favorite nightclub was, Silks Discotheque, in Emeryville. Silks Discotheque was a three-story warehouse, that was converted into a discotheque/restaurant. There were two dance floors on the first floor, one huge dance floor on the second floor, another dance floor on the third floor and two bars on the first floor and one bar on the third floor. On the first floor, at the rear, was an area that contained a few Love Seats, a fish tank, and other pieces of furniture, creating an atmosphere for private conversations. The third floor had seating at a railing, that provided of view of the people dancing on the second floor. This place was humongous, and the patrons were locals and people who traveled great distances.

At Silks Discotheque, I met women who resided in "rough neighborhoods", in the Bay Area. Women who resided in East and West Oakland, the Fillmore District and Hunter's Point in San Francisco, and areas in Richmond. During the early 80's, there were "drug wars" and gang related activities taking place in these cities. As a result of such activities, I developed the habit of carrying a loaded weapon when I visited women residing in these areas. The weapon I carried was a Mossberg 12-gauge riot pump shotgun, that resembles the one you will find in Police and Sheriff squad cars. While having the weapon in my possession, in and of itself, was not a crime, I was in violation of the law because the weapon was always fully loaded. It is lawful, when the weapon is in one compartment of your vehicle, while the bullets are in another location. For example, the unloaded weapon can be in the passenger section of the vehicle, while the bullets are in the trunk, or vice versa. I traveled with the loaded weapon in the back seat of my vehicle, and that was illegal. I felt justified in carrying the weapon, for protection. I had no intentions of using this weapon for illegal purposes.

In the early 80's, I occasionally went to a night spot known as the Elks Club. It was a night club that was located on Travis Boulevard, directly outside the gate of Travis AFB. One night, while at the Elks

Club, I noticed a woman who was dressed in white, sitting at a table that was at the edge of the dance floor. When the DJ played a song that appealed to me, I approached her table and asked her for a dance. She stood up and I escorted her to the dance floor.

When the song was over, I escorted her back to her table and thanked her for the dance. After returning to my table, I would dance with several other women throughout the night. A half an hour or so before closing time, the DJ played a slow song, so I returned to the table of the woman in white and requested a dance. When the song ended, the woman invited me to an after party at a home located on Travis AFB. She said I could follow her and her girlfriend because they knew the address where the party was taking place. I agreed to attend the party, so I got into my car and followed them.

When we arrived at the party, we introduced ourselves. Two hours following our arrival to the party, I told her I was leaving. Somehow, we entered a conversation, and the next thing I knew, I asked her for her phone number. The next day I went to her apartment and learned she had a daughter, who was 3 years old. Her daughter was as cute as a button. The first time I met her, she would not allow me to get close to her. The second time I dropped by to visit, I brought her daughter a stuffed animal. That was all it took to break the ice. From that point forward, I could hold, kiss and play with her as I pleased.

Immediately, I learned this woman was from Trier Germany and she married a man in the Air Force, who had been stationed in Germany. He was not actively involved in his daughter's life and I felt that was a good thing because I did not have to worry about him impeding my efforts to establish a relationship with her. I also would learn this woman had attempted to obtain secretarial skills by attending a local trade school, but she was forced to discontinue attending the school because she lacked transportation and could not afford to place her daughter in a day care facility. She was receiving Welfare benefits, but I could tell she was an independent woman who would prefer earning an income. When I became aware of her situation, I searched for a day care center for her daughter. I located a day care facility that would accept her in their center, at no cost to her mother, since she received Welfare assistance. Now she was able to re-enroll in the trade school to pursue secretarial credentials.

During the week, I took her daughter to the day care center and afterwards took my girlfriend to the vocational school. At the end of the day, I would collect her daughter from the day care center and hours later, we would drive to the vocational trade school, to pick-up my girlfriend. On a day to day basis, I would spend a few hours of quality time, with the baby.

The relationship between my girlfriend and I was warm, and we were compatible in many ways. We enjoyed one another's company and spent much of our free time together. Also, in a relatively short period of time, I established a meaningful connection with my girlfriend's daughter. Within a couple months, she began calling me "daddy".

My girlfriend and I have had countless non-planned memorable experiences because I am a very spontaneous person. For example, one night we were in our home and the weather was extremely humid. I turned to her and said, get in the car because I want to take you somewhere. Her daughter was with the baby sitter because we wanted to be alone. It must have been about 10:00 pm. My girlfriend asked me where we were going, and I said, "I am not going to tell you." She started giggling as we exited the apartment and headed towards the car.

As I was driving to the undisclosed location, she made several attempts to acquire the destination, but I would not reveal this information. Finally, we arrived at a park located on Texas Avenue and as I turned to enter the park, she asked me why we are going into the park. I simply said, you will see. We got out of the car and I began walking towards the park's swimming pool. When my girlfriend finally realized

I was heading towards the swimming pool she said, Terrance what are you doing? I replied, "We are going to climb the fence and go swimming." She began laughing and stated, "I cannot climb a fence." I told her I will help her get over the fence. I then climbed to the top of the fence and while straddling it, I told my girlfriend to place her hands on the fence and insert her foot in a section of the fence. Per my instructions and assistance, my girlfriend was able to make it to the other side of the fence.

Once we both were on the other side of the fence, we removed our clothes and dived into the pool. It was obvious to me that my girlfriend had never done anything like this before and she was having a good time. We must have stayed in the pool for at least a couple hours. At the conclusion of this escapade, we got dressed and repeated the process that enabled me to help my girlfriend make her way over the fence. The next day my girlfriend told a couple of her girlfriends about our night in the public swimming pool and she and I would reflect upon that moment from time to time.

My girlfriend and I had been seeing each other for a few months, when an old industrial injury flared up and I was unable to continue working. My doctor activated my worker's compensation benefits and I received 75 % of my monthly pay. At that time, my girlfriend and I had our separate places. My place was much larger and an overall better place to live, so my girlfriend suggested she and her daughter move into my place. Following a brief discussion, she was convinced my plan to move in her place was the better plan. In the back of my mind, I felt moving her and her daughter into my place would have been more of a commitment, than me moving into her place. Furthermore, I did not want to deal with the awkwardness of female acquaintances showing up at my front door. So, I decided to put my furniture and belongings in storage and move in with her.

There came a time when I really missed hanging out with my club hopping friend, Jerome, and living the single life. One morning after breakfast, I told my girlfriend I was moving out the next day. She asked me why I wanted to move out and I noticed tears rolling down her face. I told her it had nothing to do with her; it was just something that I had to do. My girlfriend then told me she does not know what her and her daughter will do if I leave them. She said before she met me her life was terrible, and she did not want to be alone again. I assured her I would still take her daughter to the day care center and give her a lift to school, every day. She began crying profusely. It bothered me that I was hurting her in such a way, but I also wanted my freedom.

After crying for quite a while and trying to convince me to stay, my girlfriend went into the bathroom. When she exited the bathroom, there was something strange about her. She was acting peculiar, so finally I inquired about her behavior. At first, she discounted my concern but eventually told me she had swallowed a pack of birth control pills. I asked her why she would do such a thing and she said if I leave her, she does not want to live. When I learned she had taken an excessive amount of birth control pills I immediately called the local emergency room. An R.N. in the emergency room answered the phone.

I told the nurse my girlfriend had taken a pack of birth control pills and I wanted to know if her life is in danger. The nurse then asked me if there were any children in the home, in which I replied, "Yes, she has a daughter." She then instructed me to bring my girlfriend and her daughter into the emergency room as soon as possible. I then advised the nurse that I am not going to place my girlfriend in a situation in which she could lose custody of her child. Fortunately, at that time, caller ID did not exist.

I asked the nurse if there was any way I could neutralize and eliminate the danger my girlfriend is facing. The nurse responded by asking me if I was living in the home and could I promise her I would make certain the child is safe. I advised her I was in fact living in the home, and I can assure her the child is not in danger. The nurse informed me the pills cannot kill her, but the overdose can lead to complications if I do not get her to regurgitate the pills. I then inquired about the complications the overdose can cause and the nurse mentioned several, including a loss of hearing. She instructed me to get my girlfriend to drink some milk because milk would neutralize the pills. The next step was getting my girlfriend to regurgitate the pills.

As instructed, I told my girlfriend I needed her to drink the glass of milk I handed her. Initially, she would not cooperate but after much prodding and yelling at her, she finally complied. Once she had drank the milk, I took her into the bathroom and told her to bring up the pills. She ignored my request to bring up the pills and kept asking me if I still intended to move out the next day. I would not answer her question and I advised her she could lose her hearing and suffer other side-effects if she does not bring up those pills. I was able to get my girlfriend to regurgitate the pills by telling her I was not going to move out or leave her.

The situation with the birth control pills altered my relationship with my girlfriend. I did not appreciate the position she had placed me in and now I questioned whether her daughter would be at risk, if I moved. There was no way of determining whether this was truly an attempt of suicide or a stunt to keep me from leaving her. Since entering the relationship with her, I had been unfaithful, and I felt a sense of guilt. I decided in the future I would not feel guilty about such indiscretions.

Several months after resuming her studies, my girlfriend graduated and received her secretarial credentials. The school offered a job placement program, so my girlfriend secured a job immediately upon completion of the program. She obtained a customer service position with a company in Benicia, California. I was so proud of her accomplishments.

It must have been a few months following my girlfriend's graduation that I decided we would move to another place I had located. I did not tell my girlfriend or her daughter we were moving until I had made all the arrangements with the landlord. It was located only a few miles from where we were currently residing. The new place had a swimming pool, so we taught her daughter how to swim. We began by putting inflatable devices on her arms to keep her afloat. The three of swam together periodically and quite often her daughter and I went to the pool while my girlfriend was at work.

Prior to moving from our previous apartment, my nights out on the town with my buddy had increased. Usually, we went to clubs in the Bay Area that were between 40 to 50 miles away, as we had done when we were in the military. On this night that I was going out dancing, my girlfriend begged me not to go. She said she could no longer take the thought of me dancing and holding other women. As I got into my Datsun 240Z, my girlfriend came out side in her robe and flung herself on the hood of my car. I told her to get off my car several times, but she kept pleading her case. Eventually, she extricated herself from the hood of my vehicle and I drove away.

I stayed out to about 3:00 am and when I came home my girlfriend was sound asleep. The next morning, I told her I wanted her to move and find her own place. My girlfriend made a few statements and began packing her and her daughter's belongings. By the end of the day she was no longer residing with me. For the next two days, I enjoyed the benefits of living the single life. On the second day, late in the evening, I heard a siren and an emergency vehicle stopped directly across the street. Naturally, I went outside to investigate the situation. Moments later, paramedics were bringing my girlfriend out to the ambulance and both of her wrists were bound in sheepskin wrappings that were stained with blood. The paramedics also placed her daughter in the ambulance. I jumped in my car and followed the ambulance to the local hospital.

When I arrived, my girlfriend was explaining to the nurse that I broke up with her and was having relations with other women, so she cut both of her wrists. When I told her to move out of our apartment, she approached the landlord and rented an apartment directly across the street from me. The nurse advised my girlfriend that she must contact Social Services under such circumstances, because my girlfriend's actions demonstrated she is not a stable person. I intervened and told the nurse that I had driven my girlfriend to do such an act by making her move out of our home. Furthermore, I stated I wanted them to come home. Since her daughter would now be in a home occupied another adult, the nurse did not contact Social Services.

From that point forward, I became verbally, emotionally and physically abusive towards my girlfriend. I had mixed emotions because on the one hand I cared about her but on the other hand I was angry at her. Analyzing the situation many years later, I gained an understanding of why I was so angry at her. Prior to meeting her I had never been involved in a serious relationship. Usually, I would end the relationship when it became too serious. With my girlfriend, the breakup became very complicated and she made it difficult for me to follow through on my intentions. If she severely injured or killed herself, it would have grave consequences for her and her daughter. Additionally, I would be burdened with a guilty conscious for the rest of my life. Therefore, I remained in the relationship.

# CHAPTER 2

## ARRESTED FOR MURDER
## MY VERY FIRST COUNTY JAIL EXPERIENCE

In early February of 1985, I was admitted into a San Francisco hospital to undergo a knee reconstruction procedure, on my right leg. Years earlier, I had torn my anterior cruciate ligament and my meniscus. My girlfriend came to see me the next day following the surgical procedure. At that time, I drove a standard vehicle and my girlfriend could not drive a car with a stick shift, so she rode a Greyhound bus to the city. We lived approximately 50 miles from the hospital. I was happy to see a familiar and friendly face, to say the very least. Days later I would be transported home in a vehicle equipped to transport patients in wheelchairs.

I was released from the hospital a few days before Valentine's Day. The next day, while my girlfriend's daughter was at day care and my girlfriend was at work, I contemplated what I would give my girlfriend for Valentine's Day. It occurred to me that making her a heart-shaped cake would be nice. I was certain a store in the local mall would sale heart-shaped cake pans, so I summoned a taxi and went to the mall.

I located a set of three heart-shaped cake pans that would make a three-tier cake. Prior to leaving the mall, I purchased my girlfriend a suit with a skirt, blouse, and matching shoes. Next, I went to the grocery store to purchase cake batter, icing and strawberries. The cake would be red and white. I baked and assembled the cake and I gift wrapped her clothing and shoes. When she and her daughter arrived home, I presented the cake and gifts to my girlfriend.

Everything appeared to be going well, when my girlfriend and I engaged in a conversation about our relationship. Then suddenly, she basically accused me of not making a commitment to the relationship and marriage entered the equation. I immediately became defensive and insisted I demonstrated my commitment to her and the relationship in many ways, daily. Then she accused me of not being very affectionate towards her since my return from the hospital. I denied the allegation as if it did not have merit.

Following the surgical procedure, I can remember lying in my hospital bed, pondering upon the injury I had suffered and the impact it would have upon my future. I was always a physically fit person and I took pride in the fact, I could do anything I wanted to do from a physical perspective. My physical conditioning enabled me to obtain employment positions that required strength, lifting and endurance. Regarding my recreational life, I have always been a physically active person. It was apparent to me that the sort of jobs I had in the past and many of the recreational activities I formerly enjoyed, were no longer possible. My physical condition/capabilities played a major role in how I lived my life, my self-image and my overall self-confidence. I guess I was submerged in a "Pity Party" – feeling sorry for myself. Why did this injury happen to me? What did I do to deserve such misfortune? It angered me that I was less than or not the man I used to be. Furthermore, my impairment brought on feelings of vulnerability because I was less confident in my ability to defend myself or those I cared about.

Unfortunately, I was the sort of person who internalized my feelings, thoughts and concerns because I did not discuss my emotions with anyone. My girlfriend, family and friends were totally unaware of what I was experiencing. Instead of validating my girlfriend's observation of my lack of affection and explaining what was taking place inside my head, I took a defensive posture and we began arguing. My girlfriend seemed to be more argumentative than normal and it was my belief she was taking such a posture because I had just undergone a surgical procedure and was wearing a brace that extended from my hip to my ankle. During this argument, she made a remark that triggered something inside of me, and the next thing I knew, I silenced her by placing my hand around her neck.

The next day, while my girlfriend was at work, I went to the mall to return the suit, blouse and shoes I had given her for Valentine's Day. While at the mall, I ran into a friend, who was and former roommate. He told me he was residing in the Bay Area but wanted us to hook-up as roommates. Returning my girlfriend's gifts would anger her, and lead to an argument that would be the catalyst for my request for her to move out of the apartment. This would be the last time we would do this dance because I informed my friend, he could move in with me, as soon as she moved out.

Just as I anticipated when my girlfriend went to her closet and the suit, blouse and shoes were missing, she inquired about their whereabouts. I told her I had returned the items because she pissed me off by accusing me of not being committed to the relationship and denying her affection. She began yelling and screaming and at a certain point I said, I want you out of here by tonight. I told her this is the final straw and she will not be moving back this time.

My girlfriend and her daughter left the house and I would later learn she moved into one of her girlfriend's home. The very next day, she called and said she wanted to come by to pick up some of her belongings. Her girlfriend drove her to my place and left. My girlfriend told her she would call when she is ready to return to her home. In other words, in addition to picking up a few items, my girlfriend intended to spend a few hours with me, which she did. This went on for several days. Even though we were no longer living together, my girlfriend continued to call me from work and we maintained an intimate relationship. We just were no longer living together.

One day my girlfriend called me to let me know she was stopping by after work, to retrieve some of her belongings. I told her I would be at home. However, following my conversation with her, I received a call from a friend, who wanted me to come to Oakland. I went to Oakland and I figured my girlfriend could gather her belongings some other time. When my girlfriend arrived, and realized I was not at home, she called the local police department. She was accompanied by her girlfriend and her husband. My girlfriend informed the officer she was living in the apartment until recently and her belongings are still in the home. The police officer told them it was lawful for them to gain access to my apartment, if my girlfriend's name was still on the lease.

It must have been about 9:30 pm when I returned home and found a ladder extending from a window on the second floor of my home. Within seconds, my girlfriend was exiting my home with some of her belongings in her hands.

A police officer was present and when he became aware that I was the occupant of the apartment, he advised me my girlfriend was entitled to enter the dwelling if her personal property was still inside the unit. The strange thing is my girlfriend still did not remove everything from my place. She would continue to come over, taking and leaving certain items and we remained intimately involved.

On February 25, 1985, I called my girlfriend and requested she come by after work to gather her remaining belongings. I advised her I was going to the Bay Area, I did not know when I would return home and I am trying to avoid another situation of her breaking into my place while I am not there. The truth of the matter is, my friend was moving in on the 1st of March, so I wanted her to gather the remaining of her belongings. She assured me she would come by after work. However, she did not keep her word and after an hour or so beyond the time in which she should have arrived, I drove to her girlfriend's home and she was sitting in front of the house in a chair. Once again, I advised her she needed to gather her things because I am leaving town. She told me her girlfriend would bring her to my home, so I left.

When I arrived at my place I went inside and turned on the television, to watch a sporting event. Moments later there was a knock at the door and when I opened the front door, my girlfriend was standing on the other side of the screen. I unlocked the latch and I turned away to return to the living room to watch the game. My girlfriend went into the kitchen to retrieve her kitchen ware and she immediately began accusing me of being unfaithful and engaging in sex with other women while we were together. In the past she had suspicions about my unfaithfulness, but on this occasion, she spoke confidently, about my infidelity.

As it turned out, her girlfriend did not bring her to my home. Instead, my friend, Darryl, had accompanied her. Darryl and my girlfriend had apparently entered my home at the same time, and Darryl was out of view, standing on the stairs leading to the second floor. At a certain point in time, he revealed himself. When I saw him, I realized he had divulged information concerning my infidelity, to my girlfriend. I felt betrayed and became overwhelmed with rage. After an exchange of words, that I cannot recall, I shot him twice, with the shotgun that was in my possession. My girlfriend immediately ran from the house. After shooting Darryl, I walked outside, lifted the hatch of my 1972 Datsun 240Z, and laid the shotgun in the back of my car. I could hear sirens from a distance and within minutes, there were several police cars at the scene. One of the officers asked me if I was armed and I told him the weapon was in my car, as I pointed to my 240Z.

At the scene of the crime, I was handcuffed, arrested and placed in the back seat of a police car. When I arrived at the County Jail, I was taken to an interrogation room. Just like in the movies, a bright light was directly in front of me. Two men entered the room, who introduced themselves and informed me they were homicide detectives. The detectives also advised me, they had requested the presence of the District Attorney, who arrived moments later. During my interrogation, I stated my friend Darryl and I were engaged in a physical altercation, and therefore, I shot him. I further stated, I had recently undergone a major knee reconstruction procedure, and was in no condition to engage in physical combat. At the conclusion of my interrogation, which lasted a few hours, I was finger printed, photographed and placed in a jail cell.

On February 26, 1985, I awakened in a strange place, lying in a strange bed and in a somewhat surreal state of mind. I pondered upon the notion I was having a bad dream and what appeared before my eyes, was not reality. However, the sounds of keys, slamming doors and loud and unruly voices quickly confirmed, I was in fact, in a jail cell for the very first time in my life. As I was rising from the bed and placing my feet on the floor, someone shoved a tray through the slot on my cell door and said, "chow". The food did not have an appetizing appearance or aroma, so I placed the tray on the floor by the door. Shortly after the morning meal had been served, two Deputy Sheriffs came to my cell and ordered me to turn around, while they placed me in handcuffs and shackles. They were escorting me to court for arraignment.

When I arrived in Municipal Court, the presiding Judge, advised me I was being charged with murder, in the first degree. Several people provided testimony, including the arresting officers, and following the District Attorney's presentation, the Judge bounded my case over to

Superior Court. Enough evidence had been presented, to substantiate the charge against me. I was taken from the courtroom and returned to the holding tank, located beneath the courtroom. I would remain there until the last prisoner who accompanied me from the county jail, appeared before the judge.

At the time of my arrest, I was wearing a leg brace that extended from my hip to my ankle. The brace had steel supports on the outer and inner sides of my leg. Due to the fact, I was medically incapacitated, I was placed in a single cell, isolated from the general population. When I returned to my cell, following my court appearance, a stocky African American prisoner approached my cell and asked me, "Why do they have you locked in the cell?" He was a muscular man who was approximately 5' 9" and he probably weighed about 215 lbs. I told him I was in isolation because I am wearing a leg brace. He then said, "Maybe they got you in there because they are afraid someone out here might hurt you". I then stated, "Maybe they got me in here because I might hurt someone out there". My remark brought a smile to his face and he began laughing. At that point I told him, "I will be out there soon, and we can continue this conversation when I'm on the other side of this door."

Following my encounter with the prisoner mentioned above, I requested to speak with the Sheriff. The Sheriff came to my cell and I asked him to explain my isolation from the general population. He informed me I was in isolation because I had recently undergone a serious surgical procedure, and he wanted to minimize the risk of me getting injured. I advised him I can take care of and defend myself, and I would prefer being in the general population. The Sheriff referred to my size and stated, I appeared to be someone capable of defending myself. Just like that, I was now mingling with the other prisoners in my quad.

As soon as the Sheriff left the quad, I approached the man who had come to my cell earlier. I asked him, "What were you saying about someone out here hurting me? Do you have something you want to get off your chest?" The man stated he just wanted to know if I was a "PC" (protected custody) case. Jail and prison authorities isolate protective custody prisoners/inmates from other prisoners, to protect them from harm or death.

Protective custody prisoners/inmates have either a sex related case against women or children, or a high-profile criminal case. When the prisoner who had approached my door learned I was not a PC case, he no longer had a problem with me.

In the county jail, prisoners may have four visits during the weekend. We can have a visit in the morning and a visit in the afternoon, on Saturdays and Sundays. These were not contact visits. Instead, there was glass between my visitors and I, and we conversed, via telephone. When my girlfriend, failed to visit me on my first Saturday in jail, I decided to contact some of my acquaintances. As soon as my friends learned of my arrest, they began visiting me.

A couple weeks later, I finally heard from my girlfriend. As it turned out, she had suffered a nervous breakdown and was in the hospital for a couple weeks. Her breakdown was not only due to the crime I committed, but also the result of detectives and police officers trying to convince her, my intentions were to kill her. Visiting me was one of the first things she did upon her release from the hospital.

During our very first visit, my girlfriend filled in the blanks. She told me she contacted Darry's girlfriend, to inform her I had forced her to move out of our place. Darryl's girlfriend immediately told my girlfriend she had wanted to tell her something about me. It appears during "pillow talk", Darryl told his girlfriend I was having affairs with women at the college, that him and I attended. When my girlfriend told Darryl, her and I were no longer living together, he confirmed I was cheating on her.

24

After learning this information, my girlfriend said to Darryl, "Terrance also is not the friend you believe him to be." She informed Darryl I had characterized him as "hen-pecked" because his girlfriend dominated their relationship. Darryl lived in his girlfriend's home and was only at liberty to drive her vehicle when she permitted him to do so. I had told my girlfriend, I had the opportunity to observe conversations between Darryl and his girlfriend and it was obvious she wore the pants and was the decision-maker in that relationship. My girlfriend told me when she conveyed this information to Darryl, he understandably, became furious. For the remainder of my time in the county jail, my visits were exclusively with my girlfriend and her daughter.

One day, during a phone conversation, my girlfriend suggested she and I should get married. There was a system in place at the jail that enabled prisoners to marry. Anticipating my conviction, my girlfriend discovered state prisoners who are married are permitted to have two-day conjugal visits. Getting married would allow my girlfriend and I to maintain our intimate relationship, while I served my prison sentence. This was news to me because I knew absolutely nothing about the prison system. It was a tempting proposition, and to a degree, I wanted to accept her offer. However, like most detainees, I remained hopeful I could possibly be acquitted of the charge against me or convicted of a lesser offense. So, I did not accept her offer to marry me.

As someone who has been employed throughout my adult life, I had the means to hire a private attorney. Following interviews conducted with several attorneys, I hired a former Contra Costa County District Attorney. As a former district attorney, I believed her experience exceeded that of most defense attorneys. I felt the skills she acquired, as a district attorney, would enhance her abilities to defend me.

Days after retaining my attorney's services, I introduced her to my girlfriend. My girlfriend was to appear as my witness at my trail and she also became my attorney's assistant. As an assistant, my girlfriend was permitted to join my attorney and I, during our attorney/client visits.

All county jails are equipped with a law library that is available to prisoners. Some prisoners utilize the library because they represent themselves in court, while others use the library to gain a better understanding of court procedures. To demonstrate how naïve I was, at the time, I never went to the law library to research case law or become familiar with the judicial system. I was under the impression I did not have to take such measures because I had a private attorney. That would prove to be a major mistake because throughout my court proceedings, in many cases, I did not fully grasp what was taking place. There were instances in which if I had understood the law and my rights, as I do today, I could have made certain objections and demands of my attorney. Instead, I had a rather nonchalant attitude about my entire situation.

Earlier, I stated I refused to eat the first tray of food I was served in jail. In the beginning, I refused to eat certain items that were served. For example, I have never cared for peanut butter. When I was a kid, whenever my mother gave my siblings peanut butter sandwiches, she prepared some sort of meat sandwich for me. (bologna, ham, turkey, etc.) Whenever peanut butter sandwiches were served in the county jail, I gave them to a guy in my quad. I resorted to buying an enormous amount of beef sticks from the jail canteen every month. I would "cook" several of them at a time, by rolling and shaping a wad of toilet paper, in a circle. I would ignite the toilet paper and hold the beef sticks over the flame. The fire would fry the beef and release most of the oil within the stick of meat. I then would place mustard on bread and make a rendition of a beef sandwich.

Later, I would come to learn dope fiends crave sugar and there were many of them in my quad. I purchased an abundance of candy bars and utilized them to acquire ham and cheese sandwiches, cheese burgers and the main entree. Eventually, I "broke down" and began eating the peanut butter sandwiches I had been giving away because I was losing so much weight.

To pass the time, I learned to play the card game known as pinochle. In the process of learning this game I met a man named "Grasshopper". He was an Asian guy who was serving time in prison for murder. Grasshopper was a "jail house lawyer", or a prisoner who is well versed in jurisprudence. He had served several years on his life sentence, when I met him. Following his conviction, he filed an appeal. Periodically, he would receive favorable rulings from various Appellate and upper Courts that required his return to the county in which he was convicted. Though he was aware of the fact, his case would not be overturned or reversed, Grasshopper returned to the county jail, repeatedly. He viewed his returns as a vacation and temporary escape from prison.

Grasshopper played pinochle all day every day, and he was one of the best, if not the best player in our quad. Quite often, I found myself playing pinochle with Grasshopper and engaging in conversation. He was a rather intelligent guy and we often had interesting discussions. One day a guy at the pinochle table made the comment that I am a first termer. A first termer is a prisoner incarcerated for the first time. It was this man's opinion that I may not know how to deal with certain prison situations.

In a serious manner, Grasshopper turned to me and said, 'Terrance, don't worry, you will fit in just fine". I did not think much of it at the time, but later I understood what he meant. During my time in the quad with Grasshopper, he had the opportunity to observe my interactions with fellow detainees. He deduced that while I may have never been incarcerated, I was comfortable around and could handle myself, amid the same type of men I would encounter in prison. His deduction would prove to be correct.

Following my arrest, I did not inform my family of my situation. My immediate family and relatives reside primarily in Eastern/Southern states. I did not contact them because I was ashamed of my predicament and I did not want to tell them I was being charged with first-degree murder. I was convinced I would either be acquitted of the charge or be found guilty of manslaughter. Since leaving home, I consistently would call my mother, from time to time. It was common for my mother to not hear from me for weeks.

On May 12, 1985, it was Mother's Day and I was tempted to call home to wish my mother a happy Mother's Day. Though I did not call home often, I always called on holidays and special occasions. I contemplated calling home because I did not want to tell my mother I was in jail and facing a first-degree murder charge. Since I was calling from the county jail, I would be placing a collect phone call. Despite my apprehensions, I decided to call my mother. As it turned out, mom was not there, and my stepfather answered the phone. After informing me members of the church had taken my mother out to dinner, my stepfather asked me if everything was OK. I replied, "yes." He then asked me if I was still employed, and I lied by stating, "Yes, I am employed". His line of questioning was in order because since leaving home, I had never called home collect. I tried to assure him I was doing just fine but I'm certain he suspected I was not telling the truth.

Days later, I called my attorney's office to arrange a consultation. When my attorney answered the phone, she said, "Mr. Hunter, the most horrible thing happened today". She went on to explain my mother had called her office inquiring about my whereabouts. Paula then explained the chain of events that caused my mother to call her office. My mother made several attempts to call me after my arrest. After a few attempts, she received a recording indicating my phone service had been disconnected. This was a clear indication that something out of the ordinary was involved because I have always paid my bills in a timely manner. Suspecting foul play of some sort, my mother contacted the local Police Department. The officer taking the call immediately recognized my name and realized I was facing first-degree murder charges. However, instead of revealing this information to my mother, he advised her to call the judge presiding over my case. When my mother called the judge, he also refrained from informing my mother of my situation and resorted to giving her my attorney's name and phone number. It was not until my mother contacted my attorney that she learned of my dire situation.

At the end of my conversation with my attorney, I promptly called my mother. Mom asked me if I was OK and then she inquired about my financial needs. I informed her I had already retained an attorney and I had a source of income. I explained I did not want to call home because I was ashamed of being in jail and I believe the charge I am facing is more serious than the one that may prevail in the end. During the conversation with mom, I learned my stepfather had suffered an asthma/heart attack and died, shortly following the brief phone conversation between him and I.

One day during a visit, my girlfriend asked me the question, "Where will they send you if you are found guilty?" I replied, "I do not know". After our visit, I thought about what she had said, and decided to obtain an answer. There were guys in my quad who were in possession of satellite phone numbers. Using the public phone in our quad, these guys utilized satellite numbers to make free and direct phone calls. You see, the phone in our quad only permitted us to make collect calls, with the assistance of an operator. Satellite numbers permitted us to make direct calls, so the person on the other end of the phone would not know he/she is speaking with a prisoner. I decided to use a satellite number to call the California Medical Facility (CMF), because that is the Reception Center that processes prisoners from Northern California, into the California Department of Corrections.

When I called CMF (California Medical Facility) an operator answered. I told her I was a college student who was preparing a term paper concerning the Department of Corrections, and I was seeking certain information. She inquired about the nature of the information I was seeking, so I asked her to explain the process used to determine the place where a convicted felon will serve their time. The operator advised me I needed the assistance of a CCI and she would forward the call. I had no idea what the acronym CCI represented. A man answered the phone, and indicated he was a Correctional Counselor I. I posed my question as to how the CDC determines the place in which a convicted felon will serve their time. The man stated, "That is an easy question. We have what is known as a "Point System." He went on to explain the convict receives a certain amount of points for the crime he/she committed, if they are under 25, they receive so many points, if they are single, they receive so many points, if they are a repeat offender, they receive so many points, etc. Upon the completion of his explanation I asked him, "If a man is convicted of murder, where will he serve his time?" He stated, "That is simple. Murderers serve their time at Folsom or San Quentin State Prison. I relayed this information to my girlfriend.

My trial lasted a week. A court order allowed me to wear my personal clothing to court. Each day, my girlfriend would collect the clothes she brought me the day before and bring a new set of clothing for the following day. On most days, I wore a suit and tie. I also wore my personal wrist watches. As it turned out, the District Attorney used my concern about my appearance against me. The district attorney instructed the jury to make note of my appearance and my attire. He referred to my well-groomed hair and clothing. Finally, he said something in which I could have never anticipated. The music recording artist, known as Sade, had recently released a hit entitled, "Smooth Operator." It was a song that saturated the airwaves. The

District Attorney told the jury to disregard my appearance because "Mr. Hunter is simply a "Smooth Operator."

At the end of my trial, I received a second-degree murder conviction. The judge made the announcement; I would serve a 17-years to life sentence, in state prison. My girlfriend, unable to control her emotions, was crying profusely. Two deputies escorted me from the courtroom and transported me back to the county jail.

Moments later my girlfriend arrived at the jail to visit me. When I sat on the seat directly in front of her, she placed her hand on the sheet of glass that separated us, and I aligned my hand with hers. It was a ritual in which she and I had performed on countless occasions. She looked at me and said, "Terrance, I do not understand you. The judge just sentenced you to serve 17-years to life in prison, and you are acting as if that means nothing to you." I responded, "What do you want me to do or say? It is what it is." As someone who was totally out of touch with his emotions, my response to the judge's ruling, was a typical response for the person I was at that time.

# CHAPTER 3

## INTRODUCTION TO THE CALIFORNIA DEPARTMENT OF CORRECTIONS FOLSOM STATE PRISON

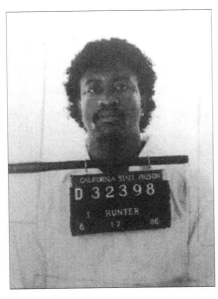

On June 17, 1986, a transportation team transported me and several other prisoners to the California Medical Facility, in Vacaville California and I was committed to the custody of the Department of Corrections. In the R & R (Receiving and Release) section of the Reception Center, an officer asked the question, "Which one of you is Hunter?" I indicated I am Hunter and he informed me I was being placed in Administrative Segregation. I was immediately taken to Ad Seg, and a few minutes later, a man who identified himself as Lt. Lewis, and two correctional officers came to my cell. Lt. Lewis informed me I was placed in Administrative Segregation (Ad Seg.), per his instructions. He stated, "The victim in your case has several friends who work at this institution, so I am placing you in Ad Seg for your own protection." Understanding the prison environment as I do today, Lt. Lewis feared staff could encourage other prisoners to assault or kill me because I had killed a friend of theirs. Furthermore, a correctional officer manning a gun tower, could intentionally shoot me during a riot.

When Lt. Lewis departed, I took a close observation of my new living quarters. A room made of concrete and steel, and something that remotely resembled a bed. I can remember peering through the window that was encased in steel bars and meshing, looking at the barbed wire that surrounded the top of each building, and the abundance of garbage on the roof tops. It occurred to me, the landscape outside my window, resembled the layout of an inner-city housing project. I can distinctly remember asking myself, "How did my life take a turn that brought me to this place?" I made a conscious decision that I would not allow my situation to overwhelm or consume me.

A few days later, a correctional officer came to my cell to inform me he was escorting me to Lt. Lewis' office. As I entered Lt. Lewis' office, I noticed two African American men seated to my left. Lt. Lewis advised me, the two men in his office had spoken to him, on my behalf. He went on to say, these men requested I be released from Ad Seg. At that point, the two men noticed I had a bewildered expression on my face, so they apologized for not introducing themselves. They then introduced themselves as Roy and Mac. Both men were serving life sentences. As it turned out, I knew Mac's wife, Luana. Prior to my incarceration I was attending college, and Luana was in my accounting class. Luana and I studied together quite often. I had no idea, Luana was married and her husband was serving time in prison. Luana followed the news concerning my trial, and she asked her husband to "take me under his wing", when I arrived at CMF. Upon their request, Lt. Lewis released me from Ad Seg and I joined the general population, or "mainline".

Mac worked in the CMF canteen and upon my release from Ad Seg, I began working there also. Mac had spoken to the canteen manager and convinced him to give me a job. My duties in the canteen included operating the cash register, delivering the newspapers ordered by prisoners, stocking shelves, and unloading the merchandise that arrived from the warehouse. My girlfriend immediately sent my first quarterly package of clothing and food. The arrival of my package meant I no longer had to wear prison issued clothing.

I could now wear my personal shirts bearing Nike and Adidas emblems, designer jeans, dress shirts, sweaters, dress shoes, tennis shoes and jewelry. There was a sense of satisfaction in wearing my personal clothing daily and during visits. My girlfriend also went to an electronics shop and purchased me a 13-inch Sony Trinitron television, cassette player and headphones.

I had an interesting daily routine while I was at CMF. In the morning when I reported to my job at the canteen, the first thing I would do is deliver the newspapers ordered by prisoners in the general population. I would deliver newspapers received the previous day, so the newspapers were always a day behind. As I delivered newspapers, I would also purchase BLT sandwiches, burritos, hamburgers and other food items from fellow prisoners who owned hot plates. After I made my rounds, I would go to the physical therapy department. A physical therapy assistant prepared a whirlpool for me every morning. The whirlpool treatments were prescribed by a physician, following an extensive knee examination. I read a copy of the San Francisco Chronicle, as I reclined and relaxed in the whirlpool.

While at CMF, I very rarely ate dinner in the chow hall. Every day after work, I would take a shower and get dressed, in anticipation of a visit from my girlfriend. Like clockwork, when the evening count cleared at 5:30 pm, I could count on the following announcement over the PA system: "Attention on the mainline, Terrance Hunter, D32398, you have a visit." On weekdays, my girlfriend would leave her place of employment and drive directly to the prison to visit me. I was in the visiting room during the time dinner was being served in the chow hall, so my dinner was the selection of food items available in the visiting room.

I spent a great deal of my time in the gymnasium located inside the institution and on the recreational yard. My activities included weight lifting, basketball, football and baseball, even though medical staff advised me not to partake in such activities. One day I went out to the weight pile and encountered an individual who was massive. I am 6' 3" and I weighed 250 lbs. This guy made me look like a midget. He was about 6' 8' and he weighed about 300 lbs. and there was not an ounce of fat on his frame. This guy was huge and chiseled. We introduced ourselves, and I learned everyone called him "Big Jack". Well, Big Jack and I hit it off and during my time at CMF we "kicked it" on the yard and in the gym, on a regular basis.

Concerning past time activities, I joined the Vaca Valley Jay Cees self-help group, that focused on individual development and Community improvement. In this self-help group, we gathered donations and held fundraisers that benefited the surrounding community and causes that involved children. We also made financial donations to the visiting room at CMF to purchase toys, furniture and other items that benefited children who visited their fathers. I also was a member of the Juvenile Delinquent program, known as "Project Last Chance." The name was appropriate because it was the last chance for the kids in the program to discontinue their criminal behavior or go to prison.

I had the opportunity to counsel juveniles from the Bay Area who were selling drugs, involved in gangs, and committing robberies and other serious offenses.

I remained at CMF for approximately one year following my conviction, to receive the physical therapy I should have received following the operation. Of course, the physical therapy I received did not remotely resemble the treatment I would have received, had I not committed a crime.

One day I was informed I was appearing before the Classification Committee for program review. I was advised my medical treatment was complete and I no longer needed to be housed at CMF. My counselor, Ms. Lopez, explained I was attending college at the time of my arrest, I have never served time in jail or prison, and I was currently involved in several self-help groups. She was presenting an argument to justify her request that I be given a level three over ride. Please allow me to explain. The crime that I committed and the amount of points I was given, required I be transferred to a level four maximum security prison. Ms. Lopez was requesting I be sent to a Level Three prison that would-be a less violent environment. The Captain overseeing the meeting looked at me for a while and stated, "No, he's going to Folsom. He can handle it." At the time, I thought the Captain's denial of my counselor's request had racial implications. As the years went by, and I became enlightened, I came to believe he denied the request because he truly felt I could handle the environment at Folsom. I believe the Captain determined that even though I did not have a criminal history like most of the men at Folsom, I was no "choir boy." He probably reserved such over rides for individuals whom he felt could not cope with maximum security prison environments.

When I arrived at Folsom State Prison, I was placed in 4A (Building 4, A section), which at that time, was the "Hole" and Fish Row." The Hole or Security Housing Unit (SHU), is where prisoners who have committed assaults or some other violent act, are placed. Fish Row is the area designated for new arrivals. At that time, Folsom was classified as a maximum-security prison. This was due to the fact, that some of the most violent prisoners were housed at this prison and practically every prisoner was serving a life or multiple life sentences. I spent approximately a week or so on Fish Row, prior to being released to the main line.

As me and the others being released from Fish Row, were escorted across the recreation yard by correctional officers, the convicts on the yard were "mad-dogging" us. A tactic used to detect or pump fear into others. They were looking for signs of weakness to determine which ones of us were prey, and which ones of us were predators. In most instances, they were staring at us from behind their 'murder 1's", a name given to the very dark black sunglasses worn by hard core convicts. Murder 1's is short for 1st degree murder. Some prisoners had the number "187", which is the Penal Code Section for murder, stenciled on their murder 1's. Though I had never been arrested or served time, I was not moved by this tactic because I have been around and understand men with this sort of mentality. I was escorted to "One Building" because I was assigned to a cell in that building. There were five buildings that housed prisoners at Folsom. Except for building 5, each of the remaining 4 buildings housed approximately 1000 prisoners.

As soon as I placed my property in my cell (Television, cassette player, food, cosmetics, etc.), I asked a convict in the building to tell me how I can get past the guard posted at One Building's door to gain access to the yard. He told me to tell the guard I need to go to Four Post to pick up my ID card. Four Post was the location where we made phone calls on the yard and received our ID cards. As instructed, I told the guard at the door I needed to pick up my ID card at Four Post, and it worked like a charm. I was now, illegally, out on the main line recreation yard. I was illegally on the recreation yard because it would take several days for staff to issue me an I.D. card, and prisoners without an I.D. card are prohibited from going to the recreation yard.

At Folsom, it was all about controlled movement. The yard closed and all activities and movement ceased at 2:30, every day. After the evening meal concluded, cell mates were escorted to the shower, by an officer and the gunmen in the building observed the escort from our cell to the shower. The prisoner in the cell in which I was assigned, was a guy who was approximately 6' 3" and weighed approximately 240 lbs. When I moved in the cell with him, I discovered he did not leave the cell for anything other than a trip to the chow hall. This guy never took showers. Instead, he took what we refer to as "bird baths", in which you bathe with water in the sink. When I inquired as to why he never takes showers or go to the yard, he said, "Man, people are getting killed out there." I did not remain in the cell with him. As soon as the opportunity presented itself, I moved to another cell with a guy from Washington, DC.

When I went out to the yard, a prisoner named Gentry, recognized and approached me. I had met him at CMF. He knew that I worked at the canteen at CMF, so he told me a job was open at the canteen on Folsom's yard. To qualify for the job, one of the requirements was the prisoner must have medium custody, which I did not. I had a maximum security/close custody classification, but I was not going to allow that minor detail to prevent me from acquiring that position. I knocked on the canteen door and requested to speak with the Canteen Manager. The first question he asked was, "Are you a medium custody prisoner?" I replied, "Yes." All the currently employed canteen workers were maximum security prisoners. There was only one medium custody position and the prisoner in this position would serve the medium security prisoners who live in Five Building.

Whereas, the day ended at 2:30 each day for maximum security prisoners, medium security prisoners could go to the canteen after the

5:00 count cleared. I advised the canteen manager that I knew how to operate a cash register and I had worked in the canteen at CMF. He gave me the job on the spot and when he learned I was being housed in One Building, he said he would submit paperwork to my counselor requesting I be moved to Five Building, where medium custody prisoners are housed. Of course, as a maximum security/close custody prisoner, I could not be housed in that building. However, I decided to cross that bridge when I get to it.

Through deceit, I circumvented Folsom's five-year waiting period for employment positions. Since Folsom is a maximum-security prison, there is only one work shift for prisoners. At Folsom and every other maximum-security prison, the work day ends at 2:30, and for the rest of the day we are confined to our cells, except for being escorted to the shower and phone calls that we signed up for, the day before. That means, there is only one work shift for a population of 5000 men. Unlike lower level institutions, in which there are three work shifts, because prisoners have movement during the day, evening and graveyard periods. I knew it would be only a matter of time before the canteen manager would learn of my custody level.

Since I had lied about my custody level, every time the phone in the canteen would ring, I anticipated a call from my counselor. Well, one day that finally occurred. My counselor informed my supervisor of my custody level and indicated I cannot move to Five Building. While still on the line with my counselor, the canteen manager told me I had maximum security status. Thinking on my feet, I had placed the chrono I received from the classification committee at CMF that stated I had medium custody, in my wallet. I was aware of the fact, that the Classification Committee at Folsom raised my custody level when I arrived.

I handed this document to the canteen manager and he advised my counselor that I am in possession of a document I received from the Classification Committee at CMF that indicates I am medium custody. The counselor immediately told him, Folsom's Classification Committee raised my custody level when I arrived. To come across as if this is new information to me, I pretended to be upset that my job now is in jeopardy. Making statements such as, "Oh, so now you are going to fire me", "If they raised my level of custody when I arrived, no one mentioned it to me", etc. The canteen manager told me to calm down and he was not going to fire me. He said that he needed someone with my skills and he would hire someone else for the other position. The outcome confirmed my belief that all I needed was to get my foot in the door.

There were few opportunities to participate in self-improvement activities at Folsom because the vocational and self-help programs were located on the lower yard. Those of us serving life sentences and considered level four prisoners were not permitted to go to the lower yard. My daily routine was rather simple. I worked in the canteen from 6:30 am to 2:30 pm. During my lunch break I lifted weights on the recreation yard. At 2:30 I returned to my cell for lock-up, where I remained until we went to the chow hall, after the 5:00 count cleared. Once dinner was served, my tier officer began making his rounds to release the two men housed in each cell, for our showers. Shower releases were strictly for prisoners with job assignments. Unemployed prisoners had the option of remaining in the building to take a shower when their cell doors were open for yard release or take their showers on the yard. While at Folsom, I also enrolled in and completed a few courses offered by Sacramento Community College.

As a canteen worker, I could allow prisoners to shop at the canteen during times in which they were not permitted to do so. As I stated earlier, Folsom is comprised of five buildings. Prisoners are housed in these five buildings and on the days that the canteen is open, prisoners housed in any two buildings are permitted to shop at the canteen. The prisoner must submit a form requesting to be placed on the canteen list, in his housing unit. With 1000 men in each building, only a fraction of the prisoners on the list can shop. As a canteen worker, for a fee, I would collect ID cards from prisoners prior to going to work or have them give me their ID cards while I was inside the canteen, standing at the window from which we distribute the items purchased. I then would retrieve the card we received from the Trust Office, indicating the amount of money the prisoner was entitled to spend. I personally would fill the order and hand the prisoner his merchandise. My ability to make it possible for prisoners to shop at the canteen made me a very popular guy, on the mainline.

My supervisors and the Canteen Manager were aware of my hustle and I offered an additional service with the assistance of one of my supervisors. For a fee, I also helped prisoners who had a hustle, by exchanging the cigarettes they received for whatever service they provided, for canteen merchandise. An individual could come to the canteen window with cartons of cigarettes, (the primary form of capital in prison) and I could exchange them for food and cosmetic items. Unfortunately, my racket would eventually come to an end, because of my pride. One day my supervisors and the manager were not at work. Instead, the Canteen Manager's boss was supervising us that day. A prisoner came to the window and slid his ID through the slot, in the presence of my supervisors' boss, who was working in the canteen that day. I should have given the ID back to the guy and informed him I cannot help him that day.

Later I could have explained the staff member was the Canteen Manager's boss. However, having the mentality I had at that time, I was not going to allow this person's presence to cause me to deviate from my normal behavior. I blatantly retrieved the prisoner's canteen card and filled his order, with a total disregard of the staff member's authority. He permitted me to fill the order and the next day, I was terminated and re-assigned to the culinary department.

# CHAPTER 4

## TRANSFER TO DVI
## MEDICAL TRANSFER TO CMC

At a certain point in time, the California Department of Corrections modified their point system. Due to a point reduction, I received a transfer to the Deuel Vocational Institution, located in Tracy, California. Within the system, DVI was better known as "Gladiator School", because it was common to observe prisoners wielding metal trash can lids to defend against knife attacks. The environment at DVI was pretty much the same as it was at Folsom, because the population primarily consisted of men who were transferred from Folsom and San Quentin State Prison. The same racial tension that existed at Folsom existed at DVI.

When I appeared before the Classification Committee at DVI, I told the panel I wanted to be assigned to PIA (Prison Industry Authority). I was initially assigned to the wood shop where the workers manufactured furniture that was purchased by state agencies. I learned how to operate several of the machines in our shop and I worked the graveyard shift. I went to work at 10:00 at night and my shift ended at

6:00 each morning. I worked this shift because I had enrolled in the San Joaquin Delta college program and I studied at the library during the day. The library was an ideal place to study because the individuals who came there were doing legal work, studying or engaged in some form of research. It was practically the only place in the prison that had a sense of order.

Gaining access to the library required me advising one of my housing unit officers, of my desire to go to the library. The officer would call the library to ask the librarian if the number of prisoners in the library exceeded the designated capacity. If the number of prisoners in the library did not exceed the limit, the officer would issue me a pass. I spent a great deal of my time in the library, preparing for and completing my college related projects. Frequently, I held conversations with a female librarian. She appeared to be intrigued by my desire to pursue a college degree and better myself. One day, she called me into her office because she wanted to give me something. As it turned out, she had prepared me a laminated permanent pass to the library, bearing her signature. Going to the library, no longer required the assistance of my housing unit officers. I assumed she gave me this permanent pass in recognition of my dedication and consistency, when it came to my studies.

My experience at DVI was totally different from the one at Folsom. The main difference was the sporting activities and leagues that existed at DVI and the gymnasium. At the time in which I entered the CDC, prisoners paid a 10 % fee every time we made any type of purchase, whether it was for personal items or purchases made during food sales. The 10 % fee was utilized to fund sporting events, maintain our weight equipment and anything else that benefited prisoners. In other words, taxpayer funding does not cover the cost of our recreational activities. AT DVI, we had uniforms for our baseball, basketball and football teams. In the back of our gymnasium, Coach Marty, had what was comparable to a Footlocker Sporting Goods store.

The area was stocked with every piece of equipment needed to play any sport, tennis shoes, warm-up suits, trophies, etc. Whenever we won individual or team sporting events, we could select our rewards by selecting anything that was in stock. Our gymnasium was better known as, "The Field House."

In addition to playing sports, boxing, lifting weights, playing handball, or exercising in general on the recreation yard during the day, we could do the same activities in the gymnasium, after the dinner meal, at night. While it may upset some people that such activities take place in prison, keep in mind that the cost was absorbed by prisoners, not taxpayers.

Due to my extensive participation in athletic activities, my right knee became unstable and was causing a great deal of pain. I reported to the infirmary and was medically unassigned from my work assignment for 30 days. After the first medically unassigned period, I once again was examined by a physician. The diagnoses led to another 30-day period of unemployment. This charade went on for several months, so I had plenty of time on my hands. Quite often, I spent my time in the library, reading and studying.

At the end of 1989, due to on-going knee complications, I received a medical transfer to the California Men's Colony. The day I arrived at CMC, I was issued a pair of pants that would have fit Michael Jackson, and a tight-fitting tee shirt. When I complained about the fit of my clothing, the officer told me not to worry because I and the other arrivals were going to the clothing room to receive clothing that fit. When we entered the clothing room, another officer arrived and asked the question, "Which one of you is Hunter?" I replied, "I am Hunter". The officer informed me someone named Sgt. Bentley, wanted to see me. I advised the officer I was not leaving until I was issued my clothing. He assured me I could collect my clothing after I spoke with Sgt. Bentley, so I complied. He escorted me to Sgt. Bentley's office and left.

Sgt. Bentley introduced himself and advised me he "runs" B Quad. B Quad is the medical yard that houses prisoners with medical problems. I was being housed on this quad because I was a medical transfer. Sgt. Bentley began his speech by stating, he was not going to have any of that Folsom and DVI "shit" on his yard. He went on to say he does not give a damn that I am at CMC for medical treatment because the first time I pull any Folsom or DVI shit on his yard, I am on the first bus leaving the institution. At that point, I asked him why he was giving me this lecture. Sgt. Bentley stated, he wanted me to realize where I am at, and let me know I am no longer at Folsom or DVI.

He informed me he does not have gang, racial or riot issues on his yard. He warned me he would know my thoughts before I have them because three out four prisoners on the line, are his. That was his way of letting me know that three out four prisoners on the mainline are informants, or as we say in prison, "snitches". I then asked Sgt. Bentley, if he was finished because I needed to retrieve my clothing issue from the laundry room. He replied, "Yes". I returned to the laundry room and requested my issue of clothing. However, the clothing room supervisor refused to grant my request. He stated, I was too late, and I would have to come back tomorrow. I explained to him that I had not received my personal property because it did not get placed on the bus, so I do not have anything other than what I am wearing.

Once again, he refused to provide me with an issue of clothing. I returned to B Quad and went directly to Sgt. Bentley's office, to advise him of my encounter with the staff member in the laundry room. I then asked him to give me a pass requesting the clothing room staff member, provide my issue of clothing. Sgt. Bentley prepared and gave me the pass I requested. When I gave the pass to the staff member in the clothing room, he threw it on the floor.

His actions caught me off guard because I had never had such an experience with staff. At that time, I asked him, "What is your problem?

45

"He did not respond. I then informed him Sgt. Bentley drafted the pass so that I could obtain my clothing issue. He simply said, "So what". I became irate and was in the process of getting belligerent, when a few of my friends from Folsom and DVI approached me. These guys had been at CMC for several months, participating in therapy programs/groups. My friends advised me the staff member was trying to agitate me on purpose. Once I get into an altercation with him, he will categorize me a trouble-maker and report me to correctional staff. To address my clothing issue, my friends provided me a few shirts and pairs of pants.

CMC was a totally different environment than what I experienced at Folsom and DVI. It was considered neutral territory by gang members, so acts of violence were usually isolated incidents. CMC was considered a "programming yard" because prisoners had access to numerous vocational trades and college courses offered by Chapman University. The atmosphere at this institution was so relaxed, that college professors from Cal Poly entered the institution and taught the courses provided by Chapman University. Even though I was to be transferred back to DVI upon completion of my medical treatment, I decided to take advantage of the available academic and vocational opportunities. While at CMC, I completed the Mechanical Drafting vocational trade and obtained an AA degree from Chapman University. During my time at CMC, I also participated in several self-help programs. I completed the Beginning Stress Management & Relaxation, Communication Skills, Anger Control, Rational Behavior and Criminal Thinking training groups.

The Beginning Stress Management and Relaxation Training was a 4-week therapy group. This group included the instructions of specific methods of stress management and relaxation training, including Deep Breathing Techniques, Progressive Muscle Relaxation, Physical Stretching, Mental Autogenic Training, Meditative Training, Guided imagery and Self-Hypnosis. The group met weekly for 1-hour sessions and practiced these specific relaxation techniques as a group, for 30-45 minutes. The group experience of deep relaxation techniques, along with a folder of deep relaxation handouts, gave participants a variety of more productive ways of coping better with situational stress through the relaxation training skills. This group made me aware of the fact, quite often we are unaware of the stress we are experiencing in any given situation.

While still at the California Men's Colony (CMC), one day, I ran into Big Jack, the huge guy I had befriended at the California Medical Facility, in Vacaville. He met and had married a woman since the last time our paths crossed. Shortly following a conversation with him, he asked his wife to "hook me up" with one of her girlfriends. Within a few days, he told me a woman who lived in Los Angeles, wanted to meet me. I sent her a visiting form, and once the approval process ran its course, she came to visit me.

The woman was a receptionist who was employed by Bank of America. After our initial visit, she consistently visited me every weekend and on holidays. In other words, she was at the institution whenever visiting was permitted. She immediately inquired about the things she could send me, so I informed her of all the items I could receive in a quarterly package. (Food, clothing, etc.) She began sending me food packages, CD's, clothing items and everything I was permitted to have. Furthermore, she was incurring train fare, hotel, and additional expenses associated with her weekly visits to the institution. Her generosity touched me. As a receptionist, I was certain her salary was not substantial. It moved me that she was using her meager financial resources to visit me regularly and send me quarterly packages.

In addition to visiting me on a regular basis, I received letters from this woman, three to four times per week. We talked about everything under the sun, and she consistently talked about God. Her letters always included references to Jesus Christ and a multitude of biblical scriptures. She appeared to be a believer in Christ and someone with a strong commitment to her Faith.

During visits, and on more than one occasion, this woman told me she was the sort of person who should have her own business. She desired to be self-employed. On one such occasion, I asked her just how serious she was about being self-employed. I then explained I had access to capital that would enable her and I to start our own business. I informed her of the industrial injury I suffered prior to my arrest and my open worker's compensation claim. I told her I could settle the claim and we could establish our own business, if she seriously wants to be self-employed. She assured me she was serious about the venture and willing to do whatever it takes to operate our business. I told her I expected her to follow through on any advice or instructions I gave her, regarding the business, and she consented.

Days prior to my arrest, I had undergone a major knee reconstruction procedure. The surgery was performed by Dr. Eugene Wolf, a renowned orthopedic surgeon, in San Francisco. Dr. Wolf's reputation is directly associated with the fact, his clientele includes professional athletes. I decided to have Dr. Wolf perform the surgery, because he goes beyond the objective of your typical orthopedic surgeon. An ordinary orthopedic surgeon is satisfied with the patient's ability to walk, after the knee reconstruction procedure. Dr. Wolf performs the procedure in a manner that enables the patient to return to the sports and recreational activities they enjoyed, prior to the injury. At the time of my surgical procedure, cadaver ligaments had not yet been utilized to repair torn ligaments. Therefore, Dr. Wolf used tendons from my thigh, to replace the ligaments I had torn.

Following the procedure, I was to undergo a year and a half of physical therapy. For this reason, at the time of my arrest, I was on worker's compensation and receiving seventy-five percent, of my salary. My insurance company was a private carrier, so I continued to receive my payments during my confinement in the county jail and for approximately a year or so of my confinement in state prison. Had my worker's compensation been a state agency, my payments would have ceased, upon my incarceration. State law prohibits a person on worker's compensation from receiving monetary benefits from a state worker's compensation agency, because as a prisoner of the state, the state is incurring financial expenses, by providing daily necessities for the prisoner.

My worker's compensation attorney was a man named James Vandersloot. He was a well-established and well-known attorney in the Bay Area. Civil litigation is his specialty. My relationship with Jim began more than 12 years prior to the time in which I decided to settle my case. Initially, when I was arrested, I told Jim I planned to leave my worker's compensation claim open, throughout the period of my confinement. My objective at that time, was to settle the claim upon my release. I realized if I settled my case, during my period of confinement, the insurance company would offer me far less than my claim is worth.

A few months prior to meeting the woman who was now visiting me, I contacted Jim and requested a face to face consultation. In other words, I requested he visit me, at his earliest convenience. When he arrived for an attorney visit, I advised him I wanted to settle my worker's compensation claim, for the maximum amount he could negotiate, and then I wanted him to invest my money in Apple stock. I explained that I am going to be incarcerated for quite a while, and the value of the money I would receive at the time of my release in the future, would be less than the value of the same amount, today. However, if I invested a lessor amount today, the value of Apple stock would increase over the years, and the future value of my stocks would far exceed the settlement I would receive at the time of my release. Jim agreed with my logic/rationale and felt it was an excellent plan. He informed me he had a close friend, who is a stock broker, and he would introduce me to him.

Jim was in the process of negotiating a settlement with my worker's compensation insurance company, when I called to advise him, I had abandoned my plan to purchase Apple stock. I informed Jim I was married, and my wife and I are going to use the settlement as start up capital, for our business. To say the very least, Jim was startled. I requested he give my settlement to my wife and he replied, "Terrance, are you sure you want to do that?" I informed him I was certain, I wanted him to give the money to my wife. Several times he asked me if I trusted my wife, and each time I said, yes. The truth of the matter is, my decision really had nothing to do with my trust in my wife. I knew it was possible for us to launch a successful business and increase the value of my initial investment. At the same time, I also realized the possibility I could lose the investment capital, if the business failed. I was willing to take the risk because I was hopeful this business venture would lead to financial gains that would be beneficial to my family. Against his better judgement, and despite his apprehensions, Jim agreed to give the money to my wife.

In addition to regular visits, my wife and I also were permitted to have two-day conjugal visits. I settled my claim with my insurance company to obtain the start-up capital to launch our business. She moved from Los Angeles to San Luis Obispo and we established a business that we named, "A Taste of Jamaica". Our first shop was located in the San Luis Obispo shopping mall.

We sold incense, clothing, jewelry, scented oils, paintings, statues and a host of other items/commodities. Eventually, at my request, she moved our business to a stand-alone shop, in San Luis Obispo, located in the "Creamery." We appeared to be making a profit and business was good. My intentions were to expand our business and increase our earnings, so I could eventually provide financial assistance for my family.

It occurred to me, that my mother could now visit me at CMC. I did not want my mother to visit me when I was at Folsom or DVI. She would have noticed the hostile environment and made note of the uncivilized nature of many of the individuals in the visiting room. My mother would have sensed the racial tension and unfriendly atmosphere, associated with level four and level three prisons. The environment at both places would have caused my mother to worry about me, constantly. In the visiting room at CMC, there was a more cordial environment.

I asked my wife to purchase a train ticket for my mother because my mother has a fear of flying. It was the first time I had seen my mother, in 13 years. Seeing my her was a bitter sweet situation because the last time I had seen my mother her hair was jet black and she was forty-one years old. She now had gray hair and was fifty-four. I wondered how much of her graying was the result of her stressing and worrying about me, over the years. It was great seeing my mother but at the same time, I could sense the lack of closeness between us, due to the years I have not been in her presence. It occurred to me that I have no idea of what has happened in her life, since leaving home at the age of 15, and the same is true, vice versa. It is sad, but I realized we really did not know one another, anymore. My mother's visit lasted a week or so and during that time, my wife took her out to dinner, shopping and they toured a few of Northern and Central California's landmarks.

The next time my mother visited me, was in the early 2000's. Her visit was a birthday gift from Bruce and Connie. One day I received a visit from Bruce and Connie. They seated themselves in a manner, that forced me to sit in a chair that placed the visiting room entrance, behind me. Once I was seated, they handed me a stack of photos. When I came to the last photograph, I was looking at a photo of a woman sitting between Bruce and Connie, on a couch. I said, "That's my mother!". Bruce said, that is not your mother, that is our neighbor. I then said, "No, that is my mother". At that time, I felt arms around my neck, and when I turned around, I was looking into my mother's eyes. Visiting room staff, had allowed my mother to conceal herself in an office. They were in on the joke, orchestrated by Bruce and Connie. It was quite the surprise. It was an expense free trip for my mother, that lasted for a week. Bruce and Connie took her to dinner, shopping and sightseeing, while she was here. Mom had a great time.

A year or so after I married my wife, my Counselor told me my wife had been arrested. I would learn she had withdrawn money from our bank account that was more than the actual balance. It was clearly a mistake in which my wife would have been aware of. Instead of reporting the error, my wife withdrew the funds. Eventually, the bank caught the mistake and requested the money be returned. My wife had already utilized the funds and was unable to return the money, so she was arrested but released immediately. In addition to learning about this situation, through my investigation, I became aware of other discrepancies.

She had been spending our money irresponsibly, and she was thousands of dollars in debt to creditors. I also learned the items she had been sending me in my quarterly packages were all purchased on credit, and this accounted for a portion of the debt she owed creditors. I also discovered she had used money from my settlement, to fly her daughter and grandchildren from Germany, to the United States. I felt deceived and this would prove to be the beginning of our marital problems.

# CHAPTER 5

## TRANSFER TO SAN QUENTIN STATE PRISON
## MEETING BRUCE HODGIN

In 1993, I was transferred to the California Training Facility, in Soledad, California. I had been endorsed for the North Facility because I had level two points. New arrivals are housed in the Central Facility, which is a level three yard. Central Facility houses the most dangerous and violent offenders and had a large population of active gang members. While in R & R (Receiving and Release) I asked one of the workers about the vocational trades available on the Central and North yards. I wanted to know if any computer related vocational programs were available at North or Central. He told me Central had two computer trades; Computer Repair and Data Processing. Upon a prisoner's arrival at Central, a Lieutenant interviews the prisoner. I was interviewed by a man named, Lieutenant Tucker.

At the outset of my interview, Lt. Tucker stated, "You have level two points and therefore, you will be transferred to North Yard ". I told him I discovered Central has two computer related vocational programs that I am interested in, and therefore, I request an over-ride, so I can remain on Central's mainline. He reiterated that I have level two points and asked why I would choose to remain on a level three yard that has more violence and lockdowns. I told him I have served time on Folsom's level four yard and there is nothing taking place at Central that I cannot handle. I advised him I am interested in learning about computers because having such knowledge will be of benefit upon my return to society. Lt. Tucker paused for a moment and then he said, "OK Hunter, you can remain at Central".

I was placed on the waiting list for the Data Processing trade. Meanwhile, I was assigned as the GED clerk, in the Education Department. My supervisor was a woman, and her and I developed a rather cordial relationship. I enjoyed working with her because she had a pleasant personality. My responsibilities included tracking and recording GED scores and maintaining files in the education department. Eventually, my name came up on the Data Processing waiting list and I was enrolled in that trade. I looked forward to reporting to the computer lab each morning because this was my very first opportunity to learn how to operate computers. My computer was equipped with word-processing, spreadsheet, database and visual presentation software. I spent a great deal of my time, utilizing a graphics software application known as, Corel Draw.

Since I had participated in a few self-help groups at CMC, I decided to inquire about the groups/programs available at CTF. I learned there was a self-help group that was only available to prisoners serving a life term, or "Lifers", as we so often are called. It was the Lifeskills Group and the group was facilitated by a Clinical Psychologist, named, Dr. Bakeman. This group met for one hour per week for 10 weeks. Its purpose was to encourage better impulse control and more effective living. Topics discussed included substance abuse, overcoming anger and aggression, stress management, forming life goals, building self-esteem, improving problem-solving skills, and re-entry; making a successful return to society.

Another interesting program at CTF, was the one known as IMPACT. In this program people who had been victimized by criminals, entered the institution to have an up close and personal encounter, with offenders. The purpose of this program was to make offenders aware of the damage and destruction we have left behind, and the impact our actions have had upon those whom we have victimized directly or indirectly.

One of the victims in the IMPACT program shared her story that resulted in the death of her husband and the sexual assault of her and her daughter. Her family suffered these atrocities during a home invasion, by several assailants. What amazed everyone who heard her story, was the revelation that she travels to the prison where one of the men who killed her husband and assaulted her and her daughter, is serving his time. Yes, she periodically visits one of the perpetrators. She said she visits him because he came to the realization of the crime he committed and has taken responsibility for his actions. Her Christian values enabled her to forgive him. She wants him to serve the time required for the offenses he committed but does not have a problem with him being released, once time has been served.

In the process of being exposed to such heart-wrenching stories, the population at CTF is generous when it comes to fund raising events. From time to time, fund raising events are conducted to acquire funding for battered women, children and other charitable causes. On May 11, 1994, I participated in the Children's Walk-A-Thon that was conducted on CTF's recreational yard. The collection of pledges and the walking of laps on the track field, by me and other prisoners and staff, raised funding that was donated to an organization that aids abused children. For every lap that participants walked, individuals in society and prisoners, pledged a certain amount of money. As I was walking the track on CTF's yard, for an admirable cause, I thought to myself,

"This is the same yard in which so many non-admirable acts of violence have taken place". The same yard in which so many prisoners have been stabbed, assaulted and shot by correctional officers. Yet, at that moment, every ethnic group was utilizing the yard and collectively working together, to accomplish a positive objective.

Unfortunately, several months following my assignment to the Data Processing program, I appeared before the parole board, for my initial parole board hearing. My parole hearing was held July of 1994. The panel recommended I transfer to San Quentin State Prison, to undergo a psychological evaluation. The panel can only recommend such a request because a prisoner cannot be forced to participate in a psychological process. I consented and agreed to transfer, even though I did not like the fact, it would disrupt my Data Processing program. Prior to my transfer to San Quentin, my wife moved to Berkeley, California, which is only minutes away from San Quentin. I intended to remain at San Quentin upon completion of my evaluation, so my wife and I decided she would move to the Bay Area.

When I arrived at San Quentin, I appeared before the UCC (Unit Classification Committee). The panel consisted of many members, including the institution's Program Administrator. The Program Administrator was a woman who was my CCI (Correctional Counselor I) when I was at DVI. When I walked in the room, she recognized and greeted me immediately. As if the other members of the panel were not there, her and I held a brief conversation telling one another of our experiences since the last time we had seen each other. I advised her of my desire to remain at San Quentin, after completing the psychological evaluation process. She assured me if I wanted to stay at San Quentin afterwards, she would make it happen.

The following day I discovered there was a vacant clerk position, in North Block. Most of the mainline population at San Quentin was housed in North Block. To acquire this job, the person filling the position had to have computer related skills. The type of skills I obtained during the few months I was assigned to the Data Processing program, at CTF.

I applied for the job that day and was immediately assigned to the position. My responsibilities included prisoner bed assignments, bed/cell moves, and a host of administrative duties that required knowing my way around a computer system. My immediate supervisor was a female Lieutenant assigned to my housing unit. However, my job also required daily interactions with custody and free staff. (Free staff are non-correctional employees)

There were many perks associated with the North Block clerk position. For example, I was not secured in my cell and my cell door was not locked, during the daily 5:00 pm mandatory count. I could stay in the office or in my unlocked cell, during count time. Sometimes I would be in the office with the Lieutenant during count, and at other times I would be in the office alone. I could take my showers during count, while all the other prisoners were in their cells. This was significant because on a regular basis, shower time, was a cattle call. There were approximately 1000 prisoners in North Block and in most instances, there would be two or three guys, sharing a shower head. So, having the option of showering alone, was great.

There was never a dull moment, during the time I worked for the Lieutenant. She was a free-spirited person who had a colorful personality. The Department of Corrections has a policy that prohibits over familiarity between prisoners and staff. Yet, my supervisors during my period of confinement (both males and females) totally disregarded this policy. As with every other supervisor prior to and after working for the Lieutenant, she and I used to talk about everything and anything. We frequently had discussions about our personal affairs. I suspect my supervisors knew they could discuss such matters with me without fearing I would repeat anything they disclosed. In our interactions with one another we both were comfortable with simply being ourselves.

I just had a flashback of a rather comical situation that involved the Lieutenant and one of my associates. This man and I served time at CTF, and in 1995, the parole board requested he undergo the psychological evaluation program, at San Quentin. Another prisoner informed me this guy had arrived at San Quentin and he was being housed in North Block. I went to his cell and he gave me an update on what was taking place at CTF, and I gave him the 411 on San Quentin.

On an occasion in which this guy was leaving the shower, he walked by the office. He closely resembled "Iron Mike Tyson" because he has a wide muscular build and was wearing nothing other than boxer shorts and his state issued boots. (No socks) The exact same attire Iron Mike sported in the boxing ring. As he walked past the office door, I stopped him and said I wanted to introduce him to my supervisor. When he walked in the office, I introduced him to the Lieutenant, and explained he is a friend from CTF. The Lieutenant asked him where he was from and he responded, LA. She went on to inquire about his neighborhood, so he told her he was from the "low bottoms". The Lieutenant informed us she used to be a parole officer and some of her parolees lived in his neighborhood. She then revealed a situation she encountered when she visited the home of one of her parolees, who lived in the "low bottoms". She said the parolee had a small son who told her to sit down in a certain chair, so she complied. As it turned out, the chair was soaked with water.

The Lieutenant then turned around with her back towards my friend and I, placed both hands on her backside, and while rubbing each cheek in an up and down motion, stated, "All of this area was soaking wet". My friend and I were caught off guard by the Lieutenant's theatrical demonstration, that accompanied her "soggy bottom" tale.

I was amazed to find there were so many self-help groups available to the general population, at San Quentin. I decided to take advantage of the opportunity to gain whatever these groups had to offer. One group that caught my attention was a three-day program known as, Kairos. In this program, a group of Christian men enter the institution to spend three days with inmate participants. This was all that I knew about this activity. I would later learn that the Kairos Prison Ministry is a Christian faith-based ministry which addresses the spiritual needs of incarcerated men, women, youth and their families. By sharing the love of Jesus Christ, Kairos hopes to change hearts, transform lives and impact the world. The word, Kairos, is a Greek word meaning in God's Special Time. Kairos provide participants an opportunity to reconsider our life choices, in hope of enabling us to become loving and productive citizens in our communities.

Kairos workshops are conducted in San Quentin's Protestant Chapel. There had been nine Kairos workshops prior to the one I participated in, which was Kairos number ten. On the first day of the Kairos workshop, I noticed Kairos members and some inmate participants greeting each other with hugs. The sort of embrace that you may observe taking place in a church setting. I was not into touching men in such a way, so I simply extended my arm and greeted them with a handshake.

After everyone had settled down, three Kairos members and three inmate participants were seated at each table in the room. One of the Kairos members provided a self-introduction and information concerning his background. Others began doing the very same. As I was listening to what the person speaking was sharing with the group, I contemplated about what I would say when it was my turn to speak. I was the sort of person who did not tell friends anything personal about myself, so I could not fathom doing so with strangers. However, when it was my turn to speak, I decided to take a "leap of faith" and be more honest than I had ever been at that point in my life.

I explained I was serving time for a murder conviction and I provided certain background information. I also revealed the poor relationship between my stepfather and I and the fact, I moved away from home at the age of 15. When I finished speaking, a Caucasian man named Bruce, introduced himself and said, "Some of us had poor relations with our biological fathers". As he was speaking about his relationship with his father, tears filled the wells of his eyes and he became very emotional. It was my first observation of a man expressing such deep feelings. At a certain point, break time was declared, and Bruce approached me. He said he felt a connection between him and I and asked if I would be willing to correspond if he wrote me. I replied, "Yes". I did not think much of his offer at the time. I felt he wanted to write me to share his spiritual beliefs and values, in hope of placing me on a path that would lead to me becoming a better person.

As the workshop progressed, I could sense the impact the environment was having upon me. I looked forward to attending the second- and third-day sessions. The interaction between me and the outside (Kairos members) and inside (Fellow prisoners) participants was great and I was really enjoying myself. Throughout the three-day workshop, Bruce and I would converse during our breaks.

On the final night of Kairos, I was walking towards the Protestant Chapel with several other Kairos participants. It was dark and there was a row of prisoners on each side of the path leading to the chapel, forcing us to walk between them. Each prisoner was holding a candle and singing a song. As we closed the distance between us and the chapel, we noticed singing was also taking place in the chapel. We could hear a multitude of singing voices projecting from the church. When we finally arrived in the church, to our amazement, the entire church was filled with men and women, whom we had never seen. As it turned out, the people in the church were members of the Kairos Community, on the other side of San Quentin's walls. While the column of prisoners on the path leading to the chapel, were members of the Kairos Community, within San Quentin's walls. They all were singing the song, "Pass It On". "Pass it on", means sharing something with others. It means to give something you appreciated receiving, to someone else. The song conveys the message we all were put on this planet to help one another. The phrase "Pass it on" means to share the blessings that you have been given with other people. It does not have to be money or anything with monetary value. It can be something as simple as smiling as you open a door for someone else or wishing someone a good day.

When the singing concluded, everyone sat down, and participants were given an opportunity to come to the lectern and speak. I felt obligated to tell the crowd about my experience in the three-day workshop. I had entered the venture with no expectations or objectives. Yet, as I stood in the mist of everyone in the chapel, I knew I was not the person I was at the commencement of the workshop. Something had changed, though I could not put my finger on it. I spoke of my mindset and attitude before and after this experience. Furthermore, I explained how the workshop enabled me to talk about private and personal matters that I had never revealed to anyone. I also confessed how shocked I was to learn what currently was taking place in the lives of the men who entered San Quentin to spend three days with us in the chapel. I learned one man had recently been terminated from his place of employment. He was a victim of down-sizing, after being employed at his company, for more than two decades. The man was approaching retirement and looking forward to receiving a pension. Unfortunately, he was terminated a few years before reaching retirement. He and his wife were living in a certain location, while his children were scattered in different locations. There were other not so ideal situations taking place in the lives of some of the other men. It was difficult to believe individuals who were undergoing one crisis or another, would be willing to come into San Quentin to spend three days with prisoners.

Upon the conclusion of my speech, Bruce introduced me to his wife, Connie. For the next several months, Bruce, Connie and I would attend the Kairos meditation hour, in the Catholic Chapel. This was a support network, in which graduates of the Kairos program and anyone else who wanted to attend, would meditate while someone strummed a guitar and quoted scripture.

Gradually, a bond between Bruce, Connie and I, was established. Since Bruce and Connie were permitted to enter the institution to attend Kairos functions, they were not allowed to visit me. The rationale behind this policy stems from the belief that if a person who enters the prison as a volunteer is also permitted to visit the prisoner, the prisoner could persuade the visitor to smuggle contraband, help them escape, or compromise the institution's security in some other manner.

Correspondence between Bruce and I ensued, and soon I would learn he was an Agent/Broker and Land Developer, who owned a real estate business, in Campbell, CA. Bruce has the appearance of a well-educated man who was raised in a "proper" two-parent household. The appearance of a man who was the product of a home in which he received proper guidance that had enabled him to make good decisions throughout his life. In time, I would learn my speculations were incorrect. I discovered Bruce was born in San Luis Obispo, California, on May 28, 1942, and he had one brother and two sisters. Shortly after Bruce's birth, his father abandoned his family. According to Bruce, he cannot recollect a time when his father lived in the home. Without a father or father figure in his life, Bruce cut his own path that would determine his fate. At an early age, he decided he would rise above his humble beginning and pursue a qualitative lifestyle that included the finer and better aspects of life. Of course, friends, neighbors and even family members attributed his aspirations to mere foolishness and "pipe dreaming.

Bruce was a very industrious kid. When he was 12 years old, he had a paper route. The next job was a door to door doughnut salesman. His product was a "spudnut", a doughnut made from potatoes. At the age of 16, he obtained a job at Ed's hamburger joint. At 18, his hamburger flipping days were over, when he was hired at an auto parts store. While living in San Luis Obispo, Bruce also worked at the Laura Lane bowling alley and the company, General Fire Proofing. At the age of 20, he moved to San Jose, California, to attend San Jose Junior College. He quickly obtained a job at Jaguar Hamburgers. Later, Standard Oil trained him to be a professional gas station attendant. He graduated from San Jose Junior College in June of 1965, and three months later, he joined the San Jose Police Department.

In January of 1966, Bruce enlisted in the United States Navy. Opting to take advantage of the Navy's early discharge offer, Bruce discharged from active duty, on December 29, 1967. He returned to the San Jose Police Department, following his discharge. In 1970 Bruce received his real estate license. For a while he was a real estate agent and police officer, but in 1972, he quit the force and pursued real estate, on a full-time basis. In addition to buying and selling real estate, Bruce has also been a land developer who owned his own construction company.

Oddly enough, it was a situation involving real estate that brought Bruce into my life. He brokered a real estate deal that included money invested by friends. At some point, certain parties involved made decisions that placed the investment at risk. The circumstances were so overwhelming, and Bruce was so engulfed with guilt, that he slipped into a deep state of depression. He was so depressed that there were days in which he could not extricate himself from his bed. Due to his state of mind and emotional condition, a friend named, Pat Hall, suggested he get involved with the Kairos Ministry. Pat said to Bruce, "I want to take you to a place where men have problems far greater and worse than yours. Bruce decided to follow his friend's advice, and as the "old cliché" goes, the rest is history. As one who does not believe in coincidences, it is my belief that Bruce and I were destined to meet one another.

# CHAPTER 6

## MY SPIRITUAL AWAKENING
## SELF-IMPROVEMENT JOURNEY COMMITMENT

Like clockwork, my wife, was at San Quentin on every visiting day. We also enjoyed the benefits of conjugal or "family visits". On family visits, my wife was permitted to bring groceries into the institution. In addition to bringing food purchased from the grocery store and restaurants, she also could bring home-made dishes. Though the duration of a family visit was two days, my wife brought enough food for 4 or 5 days. I could never consume all the food she would bring. She made a point of bringing anything that I may want or think about eating. She also would bring clothes she had purchased for me that I was not permitted to wear in prison. She really went out of her way to please me and make me happy, during our family visits. One day, I arrived at the family visiting unit with roses for my wife that I had picked inside the prison. There was a rose bush located near the chapel. I felt the roses were the perfect gift to set the mood for my three-day getaway.

The visit began on a positive note and we were enjoying one another's company. On the first night of the visit, while I was cooking, the stove caught on fire, and I used the fire extinguisher to smother the flames. I notified the tower officer of the incident and he gave me permission to move to another family visiting housing unit. When we moved all our belongings to the other unit, my wife praised me for springing into action and putting out the fire. She called me her personal fire fighter.

Even though my wife was being very affectionate towards me, something was lingering in the back of my mind. I was thinking about a project her and I were working on and she was procrastinating. At my request, my wife had approached the managers at the Longs Drug stores in San Luis Obispo, Morrow Bay and Pismo Beach. The objective was to either sell them our line of scented oils and incense at a wholesale price or place our product in their store on consignment. At this point in time, the Internet did not exist. On the Central Coast my wife was known as the "Incense Queen" because we sold customized incense. As it turned out, we placed our product in these three stores on consignment. I then had my wife contact Longs Headquarters, requesting the address, manager's name and phone number of every Longs Drug store, in California. Just as I had expected, and to her amazement, they provided this information. I then drafted a letter that I wanted my wife to send to every Longs Drug Store, located in California. My objective was to place our customized incense in every Longs Drug Store. To date, she had not followed through or carried out my request.

When I brought this situation to my wife's attention, as she had done on other occasions, she stated, "Terrance, I do not visit you to talk about business. I visit you to receive your affection." As I had stated so many times before, I replied, "Well if you did not want to do what is required to operate a business, you should have kept your 9 to 5 job." An argument ensued, and I became angry because she refused to acknowledge or address my concerns. At a certain point, I became angry and abusive towards my wife. After physically and verbally abusing my wife, I gave her the silent treatment throughout the remainder of the family visit. I was determined not to apologize because I felt my anger was justified and therefore, so was my behavior.

A couple days later, my wife and I were scheduled to attend a celebration that was taking place in the Protestant Chapel. She arrived at the prison, but staff did not permit her to enter. That morning, the Protestant Chaplain, called me to his office. He asked me what happened between me and my wife during our family visit. I asked him "Why are you asking me this question?" He then informed me staff refused to allow my wife to enter the institution to participate in the festivity because she called the prison to report I physically abused her during the family visit. I admitted to him that the allegation was true and explained what I did and why. The Chaplain made a point of telling me the Board of Parole Hearings will hold this incident against me. I did not respond because I had already considered the consequences this incident would have upon future hearings.

Later that day, I appeared before the Classification Committee and they asked me about my wife's allegations. I admitted the incident took place, and the committee suspended my family visiting privileges. However, my regular visits with my wife were still intact, because she advised staff, she still loved me, wanted to continue visiting me, and remain married. She continued visiting me for the remainder of my time at San Quentin.

There had been a few occasions in which my wife had stated I should seek help to address my anger and violence. The last time she made such a suggestion, surrounded an incident that occurred when I was at CTF. My wife sent me a variety of colognes in my quarterly packages. On a Saturday morning, while I was preparing for a visit with my wife, my cellmate inquired about the cologne I was wearing. I made note of his inquiry. When I returned from my visit that day, I noticed someone had placed water in my bottle of cologne to replace the portion of cologne that had been removed, not realizing water and oil do not mix. I was furious and could not wait for my cellmate to return to the cell. When he arrived, I asked him if he placed water in my cologne, and of course, he denied doing so. I then stated, "So what you are saying is, staff came into the cell and placed water in my cologne?" At that moment, a thought of retaliation came to mind. My cellmate had just purchased an expensive CD player and headphones. I decided that prior to going to my visit the following day, I would destroy his CD player and headphones.

The next morning, prior to reporting to the visiting room, I put on my state issued boots and I stomped my cellmate's CD player and headphones into a million pieces. When I arrived in the visiting room, I told my wife my cellmate had placed water in my bottle of cologne, to replace the portion he had stolen. I told her I stomped his CD player and headphones into a million pieces and if he says or does the wrong thing, when I return to my cell, I am going to kick his ass. My wife looked at me and asked me, "Terrance, why did you do that?" I replied, "Because he disrespected me."

When I returned to my cell at the conclusion of my visit, my cellmate had swept up the pieces of what used to be a CD player and headphones. He asked me, "Who did this to my shit?" I replied, "I don't know, I've been on a visit all day." He went on to say this is what he found on the floor when he returned from the yard. I moved towards him while taking an offensive stance, and stated, "I guess the same person who entered the cell and put water in my cologne yesterday, came into the cell today and destroyed your property?" He knew I was the culprit that destroyed his property, just as I knew he had stolen my cologne. I stood there waiting for him to make one false move, but he did absolutely nothing.

When I called my wife that night, from a phone located on the recreation yard, she asked me what happened when I returned to my cell. I told her what happened, and she expressed her relief that the situation did not escalate to a confrontation. She then told me I needed help with my issues concerning anger and violence. Of course, I totally disagreed because I felt my actions were justified.

As I stated earlier, after the family visiting incident, my wife continued to visit me and continued being affectionate towards me. The only change was that we no longer were permitted to have family visits. Though I continued to have regular visits with my wife, I resented her calling the institution to report the family visiting incident. I could not understand the logic in reporting the incident but advising prison authorities she wanted our marriage to remain intact and she wanted to continue visiting me. It would have made more sense to me if she had divorced me and no longer wanted anything to do with me. Ironically, on many occasions, my wife expressed her regrets that she had called the authorities to report the incident because she missed our time together, during family visits. When she would express such thoughts, I said absolutely nothing. I had the attitude, I would continue to have visits with my wife for the remainder of my time at San Quentin. However, I intended to file for divorce, upon my return to the Correctional Training Facility, in Soledad, and that is exactly what I did.

The truth of the matter is, I was attending violence-oriented programs, but I still had not reached the conclusion I was a violent person. Unfortunately, I was not digesting the information being disseminated in either group because I did not believe it applied to me. I was in a state of denial.

The next time I saw Bruce at the Kairos meditation session, I told him I verbally, emotionally and physically abused my wife during our previous family visit. Bruce was supportive and did not make any judg-mental comments or statement. Instead, a couple days later I received a card from him that included the following message:

> *"At times of great stress and frustration I have attacked my wife with verbal abuse. All of us are weak under the right circumstances. God forgives and loves us and asks only that we forgive ourselves and ask those we have injured to forgive us. Then we must move out of the past and into a better future just as you are doing."*

His words were consoling and had a profound impact upon me. As I read what Bruce had said about God forgiving us and forgiving our-selves, I realized I had never asked God to forgive me for any of my acts of violence. Nor had I ever asked forgiveness from anyone I had victim-ized. This revelation convinced me I had never asked God or anyone for forgiveness because I felt my violent behavior was always justified.

The following month, on 5/5/95, I participated in the three-day Alternatives to Violence Advanced workshop. On the first day, I dis-closed I had abused my wife a month after completing the Alternatives to Violence Basic workshop. I received positive feedback from the out-side Facilitators and participants. Basically, they told me change does not happen overnight. They commended me for my honesty and the fact, I am still participating in the program.

A week or so later I experienced a Spiritual Awakening. I was thankful to be alive and I recognized the presence of God's Grace, Mercy and Blessings. Suddenly, I felt an overwhelming sense of peace-fulness. It was as though I was catapulted into a state of consciousness that changed my perception of myself and others. I became aware of my connection with other human beings. That other human beings, including prison employees, are an extension of me and therefore, are a part of me. Whereas, I once believed I was different than fellow prisoners, in one way or another, I now made no distinction between them and I. Furthermore, I now had a sense of compassion for fellow prisoners and felt collectively, we are a community.

The anger, resentment and darkness that once dwelled deep within me, was gone. My perception of time had been altered. There was a shift in how I perceived time. The past and the future became irrelevant, and the present became far more important. Additionally, my viewpoint concerning my incarceration shifted. From a physical perspective, I was in a state of detainment and limited to the confines of a prison environment. Yet, from a spiritual and mental perspective, I was totally free. I made a promise to myself that from that day forward, I would serve the remainder of my time, in a positive and productive manner. I would do the time and not allow the time to do me. I decided to make the best of a bad situation, by turning a negative circumstance into a positive experience.

Following my awakening experience, I decided to embark upon a journey of self-improvement. I made a conscious commitment to take my involvement in the MANALIVE and Alternatives to Violence Project, seriously. On 6/19/1995, I completed the Alternatives to Violence Training for Trainers workshop. Upon the completion of this workshop, I became an AVP facilitator, who was entrusted to conduct AVP workshops. By now, you are probably asking yourself, "What is AVP and what takes place in an AVP workshop?" Please allow me to answer this question, in accordance to my AVP manual.

The Alternatives to Violence Project, Inc. is a private non-profit educational corporation, and is funded entirely by private sources. In its origins and philosophy, it has ties to the Religious Society of Friends (Quakers), but it is not a sectarian organization. Among its board members and its volunteers are Quakers and non-Quakers, from a diversity of backgrounds. The AVP program began in 1975 in the

New York State prison system and continues to work there. Its first workshop was held in Green Haven Prison when an inmate group, the Think Tank felt the need of nonviolence training in preparation for their upcoming roles as counselors in an experimental program in a Division for Youth institution for underage offenders. The Think Tank asked a local Quaker group to provide such training, and this was done. From Green Haven the program spread to other prisons, sometimes through prison Quaker meetings, more often by word of mouth.

For many years the focus was on prisons and the major effort was to help people to reduce the level of violence in the prison environment, to survive it, and at the same time to deal with the violence in their own lives. As time passed, it became clearer that the violence of prisons is merely a distilled version of violence pervading the whole society. People unconnected with prisons began to seek AVP training, and it became clear that the program was needed as much, or more, in the outside community as in the prisons. The first full-fledged community AVP program was offered in the small town of Owego, New York, at the institution of two local probation officers.

It was intended to help probationers cope with the problems that had led to their delinquency, but also to create understanding of those problems in the community at large. It therefore has always welcomed people who are not in trouble with the law as well as people who are, and it has made of this mixed group a single community.

The Alternatives to Violence Project is a multi-cultural volunteer organization that is dedicated to reducing interpersonal violence in our society. AVP workshops present conflict management skills that can enable individuals to build successful interpersonal interactions, gain insights into themselves and find new and positive approaches to their lives. The AVP program offers experiential workshops that empower people to lead nonviolent lives through affirmation, respect for all, community building, cooperation and trust. This is our mission. Why do we train people in

Alternatives to Violence? Because we believe that a life lived with dignity and self-respect, and the opportunity for self-actualization, is the birthright of every person. We believe that only when this birthright is made real, for all of us, will we have a just and peaceful world.

The AVP process is a process of seeking and sharing, and not of teaching. We do not bring answers to the people participating in AVP workshops. We do not have the answers. We believe that their answers lie buried in the same place as their questions and their problems – within themselves.

Our job, as AVP facilitators, is to provide a stimulus and a "seeker friendly" environment to encourage them to search within themselves for solutions. We do not talk about violence, per se, in AVP workshops. Instead, we participate in exercises that require interacting and cooperating with one another. In many cases, it is the first occasion in which many participants have interacted with another human being, in such an up-close-and-personal manner. In the process, unknown to participants, they are gaining social and communication skills.

I began noticing the change that was taking place within me, about my perspective of self, others and the world in general. When I became a Senior Advocate in the MANALIVE program and an AVP Facilitator in the Alternatives to Violence Project, my image of self, shifted. I knew there were certain obligations responsibilities that accompanied these titles, and it comes down to making good decisions. I made a conscious decision to gravitate towards the positive activities taking place in prison and stay away from the negative aspects of my environment. I became aware of the concept of "time management" and practiced this principle, daily.

# CHAPTER 7

## S.Q.U.I.R.E.S.
## MEETING JOE MARSHALL

To utilize my time in a positive and more productive manner, I joined SQUIRES. SQUIRES is an acronym for San Quentin Utilization of Inmate Resources Experiences and Studies. SQUIRES is an offshoot of the original Scared Straight program that attempted to use scare tactics to reach juveniles who were committing crimes. In this program, prisoners are trained in counseling juvenile delinquent and troubled youth. We share with the youth our own personal experiences that led to our incarceration. SQUIRES promotes honesty, trust, confidentiality, education, respect for parents and respect for one's self. The agencies that utilize the SQUIRES program are law enforcement, probation departments, special social agencies, group homes and independent parents.

As a SQUIRES' Juvenile Delinquent Counselor, I received dossiers on each kid, prior to having any physical contact with them. The kids were probably between 10-19 years old. The files revealed that some were gang members, some were drug dealers and others were involved in a range of criminal activity. When I attended my first SQUIRES workshop, I had contact with youth from the Bay Area. As I observed my fellow counselors' approach when they talked about the violence that takes place in prison, I decided to not take part in the discussion. I did not like what was taking place and I intended to bring it to everyone's attention at the end of the day.

At the end of the workshop, we reflect upon the day and what took place and the floor is open for comments and suggestions. I informed the group I did not like their approach when it comes to talking about the violence that takes place in prison. Some of the team members went as far as lifting their shirts, to reveal battle wounds. I explained the tactic they were using is not effective for many reasons. First, the youth will probably believe you are exaggerating. Second, they will have the attitude that what has happened to you or others won't necessarily happen to them. Last, but not least, they will perceive your efforts for what they are: scare tactics. When I was a kid, those tactics did not work on me and I am certain they will not deter these kids.

When the meeting ended, and the kids were escorted from the room, our meeting convened. I turned to the sponsor of our program and said, "I do not feel comfortable talking about the violence that takes place in prison. I believe there is a more productive approach we can take that will reach these kids. I suggested we meet with the lieutenant of the Security Squad and request the most gruesome photographs of prisoners who had been viciously assaulted and killed. I want the photos in which several knives are protruding from the victim's body, photos that show the results of having one's head crushed with a dumb bell, and the crime scene that demonstrates practically every ounce of the victim's blood was in a puddle beneath his body. I also want the Squad to give us a box of prisoner manufactured weapons they have confiscated from us over the years. There was silence in the room, and then someone made the comment, "There's no way the

Goon Squad" will give us those pictures or weapons. (Goon Squad is the name used by prisoners, when referencing the Security Squad) I immediately responded, "How do you know the Goon Squad will not grant my request? Have you ever made such an attempt?" I suspected in addition to not believing the Squad would grant such a request, members of SQUIRES probably didn't like the fact I was criticizing their tactics and this idea was coming from the "new kid on the block."

To persuade them my idea would work, I told them I am certain the Lieutenant is just as concerned about juvenile delinquents as we are, and he is willing to do what he can to prevent the youth of today from becoming the prisoners of tomorrow. Our sponsor liked my idea and said he would arrange a meeting between SQUIRES and the Security Squad. Since it was my idea, he decided to allow me to deliver the presentation. After making my pitch, I told the lieutenant, "A picture is worth a thousand words." Why should we use words to convey the violence that takes place in prison, when photos can tell the story so much better? Why should we talk about the weapons we manufacture in prison, when we can permit these kids to see and touch the actual weapons you have confiscated from us?

I acknowledged that some people may be concerned about us showing such atrocious photographs to children. Then I brought it to their attention, that we are not talking about normal every day kids. We are talking about kids, who in some cases, are carrying semi and automatic weapons. Our objective should be to turn these kid's lives around, by any means necessary. I told the lieutenant I am convinced the photos and weapons I am requesting will have a major impact on the work we are attempting to do. We can spend less time talking about violence and more time trying to really reach these kids through reasoning. The lieutenant paused for a moment, turned to his right-hand man who accompanied him at this meeting, and told him to give me what I needed. The lieutenant appointed that Squad member to our program and on the first day of our next three-day workshops with the kids, he brought the box of photos and weapons that I selected, to our meeting place.

I was given full reign on how I chose to present the photos and weapons. I can recall the very first time we incorporated this approach in our workshops. Before the kids arrived, I placed a table in the room. Then I strategically placed the photos on one side of the table and the weapons on the other side. I covered my display with a state issued blanket that is a replica of the blanket cowboys fastened to their saddles; a very coarse wool blanket. When we reached a certain point during the first day session, I informed the group of kids that there was a time in which we talked about the violence that takes place in prison. However, we no longer use words to demonstrate how assaults are carried out, when someone violates the prison code of conduct. I asked the kids, the parents who were there, the law enforcement officers who were present and additional attendees to walk over to the table. When everyone was standing at the table, I removed the blanket, and at that moment you could have heard a pin fall.

I then had the Squad member tell everyone the weapons they are viewing were manufactured by prisoners. I told the boys to pick up the weapons on the table. We are talking about very crude weapons made of steel or other forms of metal. I brought their attention to two of the weapons, in particular; the "bone crusher" and the "christmas tree". I explained the bone crusher does exactly what the name implies. When it strikes your ribs, it will break them. The "christmas tree", on the other hand, has a much different purpose. The "christmas tree" has the same v-shaped notches that an actual christmas tree depicts. When a person stabs one with a christmas tree, he pulls back the weapon to tear holes in your lung, heart or whatever organ he has puncture, to reduce the chances of repairing the damage. I advised the youth that CDC is not going to permit them to bring their Mac 10, Uzi or whatever their weapon of choice may be, to prison. We do our violence, up close and personal in prison. There are no "drive by shootings", taking place in here.

A couple hours later, the sponsor requested I come to his office. When I arrived, he told me to take a seat because he wanted to tell me something. As it turned out, he had just received a phone call from one of the mothers who attended the SQUIRES workshop with her son. She told him her son did not say a word between the time they left the workshop and their arrival at home. When they went into the house, she said her son turned to her and said, "Mom, can you believe those photographs we saw and the weapons those guys make in prison?' Joe would receive similar phone calls and reports of the impact the photo and weapon presentation, was having on the youth.

My participation in the SQUIRES program was a very rewarding and gratifying experience, in more ways than one. I have made terrible mistakes in life that eventually lead to a loss of life, many ruined lives, and my incarceration. As a SQUIRES counselor, I imparted my life experiences upon youth who were on a slippery slope. It was an opportunity to let them know the way I lived my life, unresolved childhood issues, and my overall attitude and lack of consideration of other people were directly related to the crime I committed. Furthermore, I also let them know I reached the understanding that no matter what happens to us or what someone may say or do to us, we as individuals are responsible for our own behavior.

It was never my objective to try to steer troubled youth in a positive direction, by using fear. Instead, I tried to appeal to their sense of reasoning. Letting them know they can choose how they live their lives by making better decisions than they have made in the past. I let them know when I was 18 years old a man said to me, "Young man, you are in control of your own destiny." Unfortunately, he did not explain what he was telling me, and I did not have a clue. At that point and time in my life, no one could have convinced me, I was in control of my own destiny or anything else. I felt there were numerous factors that would determine my fate in life, and I was not in control of any of them. It was not until many years following my incarceration that I fully comprehended what this man was conveying to me. It is the decisions we make that will determine our fate.

I always made a point of telling the youth I was not telling them how to live their lives. I let them know I reached a point in my life in which I was tired of suffering the consequences of making bad decisions. Then I would tell them, if you enjoy the consequences you are experiencing from your bad behavior, then keep doing what you are doing. If you enjoy being in handcuffs, placed in the back of police cars and spending time in jail with other men, keep doing what you are doing. If you enjoy separation from women, your family and society in general, keep doing what you are doing. If you enjoy using the bathroom in a room full of men in a jail holding tank or prison cell or being present while other men are using the bathroom, keep doing what you are doing. If you enjoy not being there when your mother or some other family member is on their death bed or dies, keep doing what you are doing. Finally, I would tell them the definition of insanity is repeating the same behavior and expecting a different result.

I would like to believe my team and I reached many of the youth who participated in our program. Frequently, we received announcements from parents, police officers and counselors that we played a major role in the positive transformations that many of the youth we counseled, experienced.

When I joined SQUIRES, I had the attitude we would be able to reach some of the youth during the three-day workshop, but in certain instances, we would simply be planting seeds. That has been my personal experience in life. The man who told me I was in control of my own destiny, planted that seed when I was 18 years old. Yet, it was not until I was in my 30's that I fully grasped the meaning behind those words of empowerment.

One morning I was on San Quentin's upper yard, after having breakfast in the dining hall. A guy approached me and asked me if I had ever heard of Joe Marshall. I replied, "No I have not." Dr. Joseph E. Marshall, Jr. is an author, lecturer, radio talk show host, and community activist. He is the founder of the Alive & Free Movement and the founder and president of the Street Soldiers National Consortium, an organization dedicated to fighting violence nationwide. He is also the co-founder and Executive Director of the Omega Boys Club/Street Soldiers, a youth development and violence prevention organization headquartered in San Francisco, CA, that emphasizes academic achievement and non-involvement with drugs. This organization, founded in February of 1987, has produced 151 college graduates, all supported by the Omega Boys Club Scholarship Fund.

Dr. Marshall is the first person to classify youth violence as a disease, and his work has been recognized in the 2001 Surgeon General's Report on Youth Violence. As Executive Director of the Omega Boys Club, he oversees the Omega Leadership Academy for academic and life skills education, the Omega Training Institute on violence prevention; and Street Soldiers Communications, which includes a nationally syndicated radio talk show. Dr. Marshall left a 25-year career in education with the San Francisco United School District to dedicate his life to understanding and eradicating youth violence. He earned a doctorate in psychology from the Wright Institute in Berkeley and has received Honorary Doctorates of Humane Letters from Morehouse College and the University of San Francisco.

He is the recipient of numerous awards and honors, including the McArthur Foundation Genius Award, the Leadership Award from the Children's Defense Fund, the Essence Award honoring outstanding contributions by African American men, the Martin Luther King, Jr.

Memorial Award from the National Educational Association, and the "Use Your Life Award" from Oprah Winfrey's Angel Network. He is the author of the 1996 best-selling book, Street Soldier: One Man's Struggle to Save a Generation, One Life at a Time.

Dr. Marshall is a trustee emeritus of his alma mater, the University of San Francisco, and a former Vice President of the San Francisco Police Commission. He is an elected Fellow of Ashoka: Innovators for the Public, a global organization of social entrepreneurs who are recognized for their innovative solutions to some of society's most pressing social problems.

As it turned out, Joe Marshall was scheduled to speak at San Quentin that day, and I was invited to attend this monumental event. In addition to meeting Joe Marshall, I also had the opportunity to hear the story of a young man who accompanied Mr. Marshall, that day. He was one of the many men rescued by Mr. Marshall's "Street Soldier" organization. The young man explained his mother was a crack addict and how her lifestyle impacted his and his brother's life. He stated, his mother allowed drug dealers to cook dope in their apartment, in exchange for crack cocaine.

When this young man and his brother were toddlers, they played with crack pipes, under the impression they were toys. When he was a teenager, he became aware of the sexual abuse and other negative implications, associated with his mother's lifestyle. One day, a friend informed him, his mother was performing sexual acts, in a nearby alleyway. The young man armed himself with a weapon and shot at the person who was having sex with his mother. Joe Marshall came into the picture through his Street Soldier organization and turned this young man's life around. The young man informed us he was currently a student at Howard University, and life was good. It was a remarkable story and it left an indelible impression upon me. I walked away from that experience with a sense of obligation, to do what I can, to make a difference in the lives of youth.

A few days later, I made note of an announcement concerning an upcoming Self Esteem Enhancement group. I decided to throw my name in the hat to see what this group was all about. If someone had told me I had low self-esteem, prior to my participation in this group, I would not have entertained such an implication. Yet, after learning about the behavior associated with individuals who have a low sense of self-esteem, I realized this syndrome applied to me. Reflecting upon my past, I now understand I allowed circumstances that were beyond my control to define me. I had low self-esteem because I never knew my biological father, I was not born into a financially stable household, and there were times in which my mother received assistance from the Welfare Department. Quite often I was sent to the grocery store to purchase food and I can recall the shame I felt when I used food stamps to pay the bill. I felt everyone was looking at and judging me.

Regarding my self-image, I am an African American who was born in 1959. When I attended grade school, the only time my textbooks mentioned people of African descent, was in relation to slavery. As a kid, I was unaware of the positive contributions that people of African descent have made to this country or the world in general. It appeared slavery represented the beginning of my history. It's interesting when I consider how so often slavery is associated with people of African descent, when in fact, people of other ethnic backgrounds were also slaves and indentured servants.

It's unfortunate that I was unaware of the benefits of reading when I was a young kid. Through reading I could have become aware of boys who did not know their fathers and had humble beginnings but did great things with their lives. I would have learned that despite the circumstance we are born into, we can rise above such challenging situations. Today, I do not carry any grudges regarding the decisions or choices my parents made. My mother's reliance upon Welfare assistance and my biological father's failure to fulfill his parental obligations has nothing to do with me or my character.

Speaking of character, I would like to share a situation that involved my cell mate, when I was at San Quentin. I had recently completed the Training for Trainers workshop and was currently facilitating an Alternative to Violence Basic workshop. My cell mate told me he was going to stab a prisoner, during shower time. My cell mate and I lived on the first tier and the "would be victim" lived on the fifth tier. He informed me he was going to the fifth tier that night to stab this man because he owed him money. Failure to pay a debt is a cardinal sin in prison, regardless of the amount of the debt. This was not the first time someone revealed their intention to assault/kill another prisoner.

In all other instances in which this occurred, I had an attitude of indifference. It was my attitude that it was not my business and if a person violated the "code" they must suffer the consequences. It was not personal, it was cut and dry.

However, this time it was different. I looked my cell mate in the eye and said, "OK, if you stab him, then what? You are going to the hole and you will be charged with assault or murder. Since you are already serving time for murder, if you kill him, you will be sent to death row. If he lives, the parole board will deny you parole until the day you die. I then covered the impact his actions would have on his family. My cell mate was one of the more fortunate prisoners who had family support. His mother and sister visited him on a regular basis and they recently had retained an attorney to file an appeal to overturn his most recent parole board decision.

At that point I said, "This is how you are going to show your appreciation for all that your sister and mother have done and are doing for you?" I then stated, "I just want you to do me a favor. When they come to visit you and your visit is behind the glass, and they are unable to touch or hug you, tell them you had to do it because the guy owed you $40.00." Now that I had his attention, I would present a solution and a way for him to save face.

I brought it to his attention that this guy owned a very expensive CD player and an extensive collection of CDs. I asked him to give me permission to intervene and approach him. He consented. I told my cell mate I would go to the guy's cell to retrieve his CD player and CDs and advise him I would return his belongings to him after he pays his debt. My cell mate had a look of disbelief on his face because my actions were totally out of character. I immediately went to the fifth tier and stopped in front of this guy's cell. He was sitting on his bed and when he turned his head in my direction, he said, "What's up T?" I said, "Check this out man. You know the situation between you and my cellmate. If you don't settle your debt with him, this situation is going to get ugly. I am advising you to give me your CD player and all your CDs and when you pay my cellmate what you owe him, I will return your property. I told him this is the first and last conversation I am having about this issue and if he does not want to cooperate, he can deal with my cellmate. He looked at me with his head tilted to one side, and after a slight pause, he went to his shelf and began placing his CD player and CDs in a pillow case. He then came over to the bars on the front of his cell and handed me the pillow case.

When I arrived at my cell, my cell mate was sitting on his bed, deep in thought. I opened the door and informed him I had retrieved the CD player and CDs. The CD player was worth at least $300.00, and the CDs were worth even more. There was no way he would forfeit the value of these items for a $40.00 debt. My cell mate thanked me for helping him avoid doing something in which he did not want to do.

This situation demonstrates the misconception that most people have about prisoners. Every day ordinary people believe prisoners are violent by nature and we enjoy hurting and killing people. There are people in prison who have this sort of mentality, but they represent a very small percentage of the men serving time. In many instances, when a prisoner assaults/kills a prisoner or even a staff member, he is doing what is expected of him. If he is affiliated with a group, it is mandatory he maintains a certain image and represent his associates.

If a prisoner allows someone to violate the code of conduct in prison and does nothing about it, he appears to be weak. If he is affiliated, his affiliates appear to be weak. I presented a way out for my cell mate and he accepted it. It was an opportunity for him to save face because he can tell everyone he was going to stab this individual, but I stepped in. In other words, it was not his decision to not follow through on his plans to stab this man; it was my intervention that prevented him from carrying out his initial intent.

I can still remember how I felt when I prevented that assault from taking place. For the first time, I acted in the capacity of a mediator, instead of an instigator. I knew it had everything to do with what I had learned in my self-help groups, and my return to the spiritual values I had acquired, during my childhood years. A time when I attended church regularly, with my family.

Eventually, my cell mate and I transferred from San Quentin and returned to the Correctional Training Facility (CTF), in Soledad, CA. Upon my return, I appeared before the UCC and requested to be reassigned to the Data Processing Vocational Trade, so I could complete the program. In a relatively short period, I was once again in the computer lab, learning how to utilize word-processing, database, spreadsheet and visual presentation software. I looked forward to reporting to this assignment, each day.

As I indicated earlier, the Board of Parole Hearings requested I transfer to San Quentin to undergo a psychological evaluation. When I returned to CTF I appeared before the BPH and received a three-year denial of parole. The panel of commissioners indicated I was denied parole because I assaulted my wife during the family visit at San

Quentin. A three-year denial meant I would not appear before the BPH for a parole suitability hearing, until the year 1998.

Shortly after appearing before the parole board, Bruce advised me he and Connie could visit me because the Kairos Ministry does not exist at CTF. I sent them visiting forms and upon their approval, they traveled to Soledad, for a visit. Bruce and Connie visited me periodically, and I spoke with them weekly, via telephone. With the passing of time, I found myself getting more comfortable with Bruce and Connie, as far as personal matters that I had never shared with anyone. When I think about the relationships I had with people prior to my confinement, they really cannot be defined as relationships. If someone were to speak with people who considered me a friend, they could not tell them anything personal about me. It eventually occurred to me that revealing matters that I formerly was ashamed to tell anyone, proved to be the impetus that made the bond between Bruce, Connie and I, possible. The more transparent I became, it appeared their love and concern for me became stronger.

In Alternatives to Violence workshops, our objective is to create a safe environment that will enable participants to share thoughts and feelings that they normally would not discuss with anyone. I believe that is what happened between Bruce, Connie and me. We established a bond and friendship between us that gave me a sense of feeling safe enough to trust and share anything with them. This would prove to be the critical factor that enabled me to make the most of my participation in self-help groups, across the board.

In addition to visiting me and paying for my weekly collect phone calls, Bruce and Connie sent me quarterly packages, books of stamps and money orders on my birthday and at Christmas. In a relatively short period, they began sending me birthday and holiday greeting cards that addressed me as their son. They went out of their way to let me know I was a member of their family. As a matter of fact, when their son Dan, graduated from high school, he accompanied Bruce on a visit. Dan was 18 years old at the time and he had just enrolled at Gonzaga University. Dan, Bruce and I interacted and conversed with one another throughout our 6 or 7-hour visit. Dan informed me he was majoring in accounting, with the intention of becoming a CPA.

A couple hours after the visit had ended, I called Bruce. I always made a point of calling him and Connie, hours following our visits, to make certain they made it home safely. When I called Bruce, he let me know that as him and Dan left the visiting room, he asked Dan what he thought of me. He said Dan thought I was an intelligent and well-informed individual. Bruce then revealed the purpose behind bringing Dan to the institution to meet me. Bruce told me he asked Dan to do him a favor. Bruce asked Dan to continue the relationship that exists between Bruce and I, should anything happen to Bruce. Dan agreed to maintain a friendship with me, if anything happened to his father. Of course, I could not believe what he told me, and I remember telling my mother about this agreement between Bruce and his son, the next time I spoke with her.

# CHAPTER 8

## BEFRIENDING WILLIE RUFF

In the summer of 1996, I tuned in to a PBS presentation that would prove to be a blessing, in more ways than one. The title of the presentation was, "Pass It On", and it was a documentary about two Black musicians, named Willie Ruff and Dwike Mitchell. What is ironic is the title of the presentation (Pass It On) shares the name of the song the Kairos community was singing, on the final night of the Kairos workshop. Willie Ruff plays the French horn and stand-up bass and Dwike Mitchell is a pianist. At the outset of the presentation, Ruff and Mitchell were entering an inner-city grade school. Willie had his French horn and bass, and Mitchell utilized the school's piano, located in the school's music room. Willie asked a little African American girl who must have been about 8 or 9 years old, to play Mary Had a Little Lamb, on the piano. When she was finished, Willie told her he would demonstrate the meaning of improvisation, by converting Mary Had a Little Lamb into a jazz composition. The children were amazed at what they had just witnessed. The documentary highlighted the work Ruff and Mitchell were doing to introduce inner-city children to jazz and music. Their intention was not only to inspire children, but also make them aware of the many possibilities, that life offers all of us.

I was so touched by this presentation that I decided to write the producer to express my gratitude of viewing this documentary. Unfortunately, the credits did not include the producer's identity. However, I recalled during the presentation, it was mentioned that Willie Ruff was a music professor at Yale University. Therefore, I went to the institution library to obtain the address for Yale. Upon acquiring the address, I wrote Mr. Ruff a letter. I informed him I had viewed "Pass It On", from my prison cell. I expressed the pleasure I derived from viewing a presentation that portrayed two African American men, in such a positive light. Very rarely will one find anything on television that depicts the positive actions of African American men, yet, you can turn to any television station at any given time and find the reporting of our negative behavior.

I commended him and Mitchell for the work they are doing in the inner-city, where so many kids are residing in homes in which the father is absent. I let him know that many of the men in prison, including myself, never knew our biological fathers, or enjoyed the benefit of having a father-figure in our lives. I said much more, and the letter was a couple pages in length. I did not expect a reply, I simply felt compelled to speak my mind. To my amazement, a week or so later, a letter from Willie Ruff arrived. The following is what he stated in his letter, verbatim.

*Dear Mr. Hunter,*

*"Your letter arrived a week or so ago and I thank you for your warm word and encouragement. We received a lot of mail and phone calls in response to the documentary you saw— "Pass It*

*On." In fact, the letters and calls continue coming in, but yours gave us more encouragement than all the others.*

*A lot of work and trouble went into making the program and there were times, many actually, when Mitchell and I wondered if the end result would be worth the effort. You answered that question for us with your letter, for if only one person was touched enough to write the letter you wrote, then it was clearly worthwhile.*

*I took the liberty of sending a copy of your letter to the producer and staff at Oregon Public Television because I thought they would be encouraged too after all the work. I also read the letter to a friend in New York via telephone and she said, "The man is a writer." I agree; you are.*

*I see you write on a computer as I do. I encourage you to keep writing every day if that is possible.*

*I enclosed a copy of my book, an autobiography which I hope you will find interesting. Again, many thanks for writing, and all best to you and your family."*

*Most Sincerely,*
*Willie Ruff,*
*Professor of music*

As stated in Willie's letter, he forwarded me a copy of his autobiography, entitled, "A Call to Assembly." In the process of reading this book I acquired a deep sense of respect and admiration for a man who has truly lived a remarkable life. His book made me conscious of those who have lived their lives in a way in which, they enjoyed wonderful relationships with other people, and left some sort of legacy behind. People whom when they pass away, many will travel extensive distances to pay their final respects. While their physical presence will be missed, they will forever live in the hearts and minds of those whose lives were impacted by them. When I reached this level of consciousness, I became so ashamed of the way I have lived my life. I squandered all the opportunities that came my way that presented the chance for me to do something meaningful. Please allow me, to share a fraction of what I learned about Willie.

Willie was born on Labor Day, in 1931, in a town known as, Sheffield. Sheffield is the heart of Muscle Shoals, Alabama. His father abandoned him and his mother one year after Willie was born. Fortunately, the strongest learning advocate to touch his life, besides his mother, was a man he affectionately called, "Daddy Long." Only Willie called him Daddy Long. To everyone else, he was "Uncle Henry" or "Mister Long." It is crystal clear, that Daddy Long was a father figure that played a major role in Willie's early development.

Willie had seven siblings and the eight of them were fathered by four different men. In his autobiography, Willie states, "Though her eight children were born of four different fathers, she was, for us all, our blood link and the centerpiece of our world." His mother Manie Carolyn Broaden, escaped a brutalizing hard-drinking husband, who fathered her first child when she was 16 years old. When she moved to Sheffield, she married her second husband, Mr. Autry Broaden, whom his mother referred to as the best of the men in her life. However, a year after their marriage and shortly after the birth of their baby, Mary Louise, Mr. Broaden was shot to death, by Sheffield's Police. The police said it was a case of mistaken identity. So, with one more infant to care for, Willie's mother pressed on, alone and in worse straits than before.

At the age of two, Willie began singing in local grocery stores, for candy. A mile-long bridge connects Sheffield with the town of Florence, where high upon a scenic bluff sits the birthplace of W.C. Handy, the "Father of the Blues." When Willie was in the second grade, his teachers, Mrs. and Dr. Coker, persuaded the "Father of the Blues", on one of his frequent trips from New York back to his hometown, to bring his trumpet to Willie's school, to play and talk to the children.

As requested of him, W.C. Handy did talk to Willie and the other children. He said, "It is from the spiritual, that all else in our musical story in America took root." He demonstrated "Go Down Moses' and "Swing low, Sweet Chariot" on his trumpet and showed the children those qualities that our sacred music shares with the blues and jazz. His musical examples were so clear and easy to follow, and his words were so strong, that Willie knew he was on the receiving end of a precious gift. W.C. Handy was passionate about the music's worth and admonished the children to always value all the rich legacy of our ancestry, the secular and the sacred alike. He said, "Be proud of it and hold it up. Sing it with thanksgiving in your hearts, and with pride and dignity in your voices." Willie felt his words were aimed directly at him, and he knew they would stay with him always.

After Mr. Handy's visit to Willie's school, his musical horizon's broadened, from singing at the grocery store for candy, to ownership of a snare drum and a pair of drumsticks. The drum, the sticks and Willie's first music lessons were gifts from a white boy, Mutt McCord, his neighbor and major early musical influence. A warm lifelong friendship developed from the lessons Willie received from Mutt. When Mutt felt Willie was ready, he began explaining the intricacies of ensemble work in big band drumming and why it was important for the drummer to be able to read the music and know what all the instruments in the orchestra doing. To get his point across, Mutt introduced Willie to the music of Duke Ellington, Count Basie, Benny Goodman and Jimmie Lunceford.

Willie came home from school one day in the early spring of 1944 and found his mother alone and resting in bed. It appeared there was a spot on her lung. In 1994, "a spot on the lung" was TB-the kiss of death for 15 out of every 1000 African Americans from the south. Her doctor, Dr. Littlepage, advised a trip to Meharry Medical College, in Nashville, because that was the South's only training hospital for Negro doctors. The trip to Meharry proved to be futile, so Willie's mother returned home, and everyone did all they could do to make her as comfortable as possible.

Willie lost his mother on April 12, 1945. She was forty-five and Willie was thirteen years old. After his mother's death, Willie contemplated finishing school, while living with his father, Red Ruff. His father was living in Evansville, Indiana at the time. Willie liked the idea of moving North, but he really knew very little about his father. The most he could remember about his father, is that in his preschool years, he occasionally came riding into Sheffield on freight trains late at night, to visit him. But his father never stayed more than a day or two. For a short period, when Willie was younger, he lived with his father and his new wife, in Tupelo, Mississippi. His father agreed to let him come to Evansville, Indiana to finish high school. His father was now a bachelor, making rooming houses a way of life. Red Ruff came to Sheffield in his coal hauling truck to transport Willie, his piano and drums, to Indiana. He stated, "We got us a nice room in a place close to the school."

At Evansville's Lincoln High School, Willie signed up for every music activity available. He played the snare drum in the marching band, became the choir's first tenor, and every day he played his boogie and blues on the piano, during recess. An older boy at school, Milton Lambert, played the piano and could read classical music. He read music like a professional and he played every piece of sheet music he could find by Fats Waller and Duke Ellington. Milton and Willie became good friends and they played boogie woogie duets. Soon, Milton, his brother Robert and Willie formed a band. The band experienced success and earned money for a while, but unfortunately, disbanded. Milton's grandmother, a fierce church woman discovered Milton and

Robert were playing nonreligious music. The brothers had to quit playing jazz music to please their grandmother.

Early one morning in Evansville, Willie had a discussion with Arthur Rucker, the younger brother of his Uncle Grover's wife. Arthur was now a big-time soldier in the Army. He explained all the benefits associated with being in the Army, including the opportunities for musicians. Willie told Arthur he is only 14 and did not believe he could convince a recruiter he was 17 years old. Arthur planted the seed that Willie could sign the parental permission form himself, and no one would be the wiser. That same afternoon, Willie picked up a parental permission form from the recruiter's office, forged his father's name and had the document notarized by the neighborhood grocer. The grocer signed and stamped the forgery while weighing a sack of onions, with never making note of the content of the document. The night before Willie departed for boot camp, he informed his father of his desire to enlist, and his father consented to allowing him to do so.

Following his re-enlistment in the Army, in 1947, Willie received orders to report to a base called Lockbourne, in Columbus, Ohio. Willie became a member of the only band in the entire Air Corps, for African Americans. To improve his skills and better serve the band, he found a teacher named Abe Kniaz, a French hornist in the Columbus Philharmonic Orchestra. During Willie's musical apprenticeship in the Army, he was a member of several all African American military bands. Along the way, he met numerous individuals who aided him in his pursuit to become a musician. However, Willie taught himself how to play the French horn, and with the assistance of his duo partner, Dwike Mitchell, he also taught himself how to play the stand-up bass.

Willie is a graduate of Yale's School of music and he eventually became a professor with tenure, at Yale. He has enjoyed a musical career in which he has played with countless jazz greats, including Lionel Hampton and Duke Ellington. His accomplishments are too vast, to recount them all. In June of 1959, the Yale Russian Choir and the Ruff – Mitchell duo, left New York for Europe. To enable him to introduce jazz music and tell jazz's story to Russians, Willie learned the Russian language months before his departure. On June 2nd, 1981, Dwike and Willie were in Shanghai, at China's oldest conservatory. Several hundred students were waiting to hear their first American jazz concert. Willie also would deliver his first lecture in Chinese. For two solid years, prior to his trip to China, Willie had been strenuously studying Mandarin.

After reading Willie's autobiography, I wrote him a letter expressing how much I enjoyed reading about the life he has lived and his many experiences. He wrote back and that was the beginning of an ongoing friendship. Over the years, he would keep me apprised of what was going on in his life, and I would do the same.

Willie truly became a friend, who always offered me a word of encouragement. To illustrate the relationship between Willie and me, the following is a letter I received from him on November 5, 1997. He had just received a birthday card that I designed for him, using Corel Draw software.

*Dear Terrance:*

*"Many thanks for your fabulous birthday greeting. It was great, graphics, music and all. Congratulations, too, on the calculations through which you deduced the date of my sixty-six.*

*Things are busy here at Yale after a full summer of working in Alabama daily on another book and new music to record with Mitchell, my partner in the duo. I was very pleased to learn that you, too, are blessed with "good health, high spirit, and what you perceive to a sound frame of mind.*

*I will keep the birthday card you made me with sincerest hopes that the future will hold good health and the best of great things for you and yours".*

*With warmest best wishes,*
*Willie Ruff*

Willie wrote the next letter, on August 9, 1998, after returning from a trip to Cuba. The objective of his trip was to make the musical connection between West Africa, North America and Cuba.

*Dear Terry:*

*"I owe you a ton of apologies for taking so long to respond to the many elegant cards you've made and sent me — the last arriving close to Father's Day. They have all come at good times and my only excuse for taking so long to let you know I got and appreciate them is lack of time.*

*Firstly, I have been on leave from Yale all year, traveling and trying to finish the book I mentioned to you earlier. This is a very complicated project that is beyond my literary powers. But since nobody else can tell the story I'm trying to convey, I have to try it and pray for Divine intervention, which fortunately, I have with growing abundance. No work I've ever attempted has required the kind of seven-days-a-week, dogged and tough hard work and I only hope it will be useful in making sense of how America feels about her culture.*

*I write you from Alabama where I have been all summer, arriving here after having spent a couple of rewarding weeks in Cuba searching for remnants of the great West African drumming and language traditions that survived their slavery system. In spite of the eradication of those practices in North America, strong kinships abound between the Afro-Cuban and his North American counterpart.*

*Dizzy Gillespie, of course, knew and demonstrated this fact in his ground-breaking music. Cuba and its music is not a part of my new book, the study trip was just a way of doing something nice for my ears.*

*Terry, I hope and pray that you are thriving, and that your spirit will remain strong and optimistic. I wish the best to your family and especially hope the future will bring you and them many rewards, joy, and lots of peace.*

*And know that if I am late in getting word back to you, it is only because I'm so much on the go with a lot to get done before I retire from teaching in four or five years. It is an old story with me, but I still seem to be making up for lost time."*

*Til next time, my friend*
*Ever, Willie*

Willie wrote the below letter, on March 27, 2001, informing me of his current project which involved the Buffalo Soldiers participation in the Spanish-American War. He mentions he sent my nieces music CDs recorded by him and Dwike Mitchell, and the fact, I received the Warden at CTF's approval, for Willie to donate his CDs and books he had written, to the institution's library.

*Terrance!*

*"It seems I am always writing you from airport terminals. I am thankful for the laptop computer. It makes possible this tardy response to your mail from the last Xmas holidays.*

*Been in Alabama for Yale's spring break for two weeks work-ing on the old house, old truck and unkempt grounds, and now back to the grind of putting on a huge concert with local New Haven kids performing at Yale, lots of them.*

*By now you will have had notice – I hope – that Denise Meyer, my website manager, has sent CDs and a book to your wonderful nieces. And thank you for the lovely photos of them; I can see why you are so proud and so full of hope for them. Denise also said she would ask you if CDs or books could be donated to the library there. I trust she did and that the answer was yes.*

*Since last I wrote you, I took a trip to Cuba to retrace the Spanish-American war of 1898 in which so many Black "Buffalo Soldiers" fought with conspicuous valor. You will recall from "A Call to Assembly" that some of my own music teachers in the Army were themselves protégées of musical men who had fought in Cuba. So my trip was to famous San Juan Hill and other battlefields in and around Santiago.*

*My goal is to write a photo essay giving little known history of our men's experience there. (Even the Cubans didn't know that the U.S. 9th and 10th Cavalry, and the 24th and 25th Infantries whose unit names are prominent on monuments around Santiago, were Black soldiers). Now they know, for I put them straight. And I am finding some interesting photos of those units taken in Cuba. They will round out my essay.*

*Oh, another unfinished business detail. Your friend Bruce sent me a very nice email which vanished from my laptop before I could respond to it – sometimes I don't get to check for weeks---. Please tell him what happened and that I would appreciate another to which I will respond. His message was mostly to welcome me to the family of your ad-mirers, and I appreciated it, tell him.*

*Also, I liked the position you took in the discussion you had on why our people are not actively involved in broad-er social issues, in progress and uplift of every sort. In my own small way, I am seeing small but potent openings to broach such discussions everywhere I go. Perhaps our time approaches.*

*My best to Sartuce, and thanks for letting him see my letter as you give him my best. As I get ready to hop on the plane to New Haven, I begin the letter to your nieces here from Washington D.C. again.*

*P.S. From New Haven: Just got word from Denise that CDs and books have been OK'ed for your library. I will fin-ish the letter to the "Hairston sisters" in the next few days introducing myself,*

*All best, good friend,*
*Willie*

# CHAPTER 9

## COMPUTERS FOR KIDS
## GRANDMA LOUISE

I graduated from the Data Processing vocational trade, on April 24, 1997. One of the primary objectives of the Data Processing program is to train prisoners for prison clerical positions. In most cases, graduates of the program seek clerical jobs, so they can earn an income. I was not interested in using my computer skills in a job situation at that time, so upon completion of the program, I enrolled in the Computer Refurbishing vocational trade. I wanted to learn as much as I could about hardware and software.

A company known as Detweiler, sponsored the Computer Refurbishing program. Detweiler provided our computer parts and software. In the Computer Refurbishing program, I learned how to assemble, repair, upgrade and refurbish desk top computer systems. Furthermore, I also became skillful at installing and running diagnostic software applications. Initially, students are on the classroom side of the program for training. Once we acquire the necessary skills, we can move to the production side of the program. Our objective was to provide computers systems and software for K-12 schools throughout California that were under funded and could not afford to purchase computers for their students. K-12 school officials could contact our sponsor in request of computers and software. We would build the systems, load the appropriate customized software, and ship the systems to the schools, at absolutely no cost to them.

We received thank you cards from kids who received our computers. We taped these cards to the molding below the ceiling. It was amazing that these kids thanked us in such heart-warming manners, despite knowing we were prisoners and their computers came from a prison. Their kind words gave the technicians in my shop a sense of giving back and making a difference, even though we were serving prison terms. I often wondered about the number of kids who had access to the systems we built, upgraded, repaired and refurbished, as I gazed at the thank you cards in our shop.

In 1998 I appeared before the parole board and once again, received a three-year denial of parole. As was the case at my hearing three years earlier, the panel indicated the domestic violence incidence at San Quentin was the cause of my denial of parole. One major benefit that I derived from my participation in self-help groups was my transformation from an emotional person to a more logical and rational human being. I reached a point in which I did not take the results I received at parole board hearings, personal. Instead, I owned and took responsibility for the results I was receiving because the results were based upon my behavior. Therefore, despite my disappointment of the results of parole hearings, I was able to leave my hearings and resume my daily routine. On the other hand, what disturbed me the most was informing my friends and loved ones, the parole board had denied me parole. Year after year, my supporters submitted letters that indicated the many forms of support they would provide upon my release, to no avail.

Fellow prisoners would question my continued participation in self-help and positive activities because the parole board continued to find me unsuitable for parole. Many of my associates would bring it to my attention, the parole board was granting parole to men partaking in self-help groups that I facilitated, while the board continued to deny me parole. In response to such inquiries, I would explain I do not participate or facilitate self-help groups because I believe my actions will lead to my release from prison. I participate in self-help groups because I choose to gravitate towards the positive activities in prison and now that I have addressed my own demons, I feel obligated to do what I can to help others. Throughout my years of parole denials, I continued to facilitate AVP, Anger Management, Cognitive Behavior, Life Skills, and a host of additional self-help groups.

In June of 2001, a tragedy occurred while my dear friends, Bruce and Connie were on a Caribbean Cruise. When they returned from the cruise, I called them to confirm they had made it home safely. Connie answered the phone and the first thing she said was, "Terrance, I have some bad news". She informed me people tried to contact her and Bruce while they were away on the cruise, but those calls did not get through. Connie's father Sam was in the hospital. It appeared he suffered a ruptured gall bladder. When our phone conversation ended, I went to the cell of a friend in request of one of his customized greeting cards. I emphasized the card must go out with the following morning's mail. His name is Preston, and he had all the material to make special, quality greeting cards. I would have preferred making the card myself, but I did not have access to my computer at that time, so I had to outsource the job. I told Preston my friend's father is ill, in the hospital, and that I need a get-well card. I knew Connie's father, Sam, is a devout Catholic, so I told Preston to place a bible on the front of the card, and I provided the wording for the outside and inside portion of the card. He said I could pick up the card in a couple hours.

Two hours later, I went to Preston's cell to pick up the card for Sam. Bruce and Connie had recently sent me a quarterly package that contained cans of fried dace, which is a small freshwater fish of the minnow family. A friend noticed the five cans of fried dace in my hands and asked me what I intended to do with them. I explained I was giving them to Preston in exchange for a greeting card I requested. My friend then stated, give me the five cans of fried dace and I'll give you five cans of tuna that you can give to Preston. I then informed him that I have five cans of tuna that I could give to Preston, but to show my appreciation of his work I am giving him something in which I know he will enjoy receiving. I was very pleased with the card and I addressed it to Connie and placed it in the mail that night.

A couple days later, Connie received the card. When she visited her father that day, she gave him the card. Sam asked Connie, "Who sent the card", and she said, "The card is from Terrance, the man Bruce and I visit in prison". Connie used a piece of tape and fastened the card to one of the walls in her father's hospital room. When Connie's mother, Louise arrived, she inquired about the card and Connie informed her it was from me. A few days later, I received a letter from someone named Louise Bosco. The envelope contained a thank you card and a book of stamps. The card contained a message from Louise Bosco, thanking me for sending her husband such a lovely get-well card. In response to Louise's card, I approached Preston in request of a thank you card for Louise.

In addition to thanking her for sending me the thank you card and stamps, I also included a wish that God would grant her family the strength to endure her husband's ordeal. The next thing I knew, Louise and I were corresponding on a regular basis. There was a quick turn around on our letters because both she and I were responding immediately, to one another's missives. One day I learned Sam had fought the good fight, but on October 12, 2000, he passed away. Louise and I continued to correspond. She sent me cards on my birthday and every holiday. On a regular basis, she would send me greetings cards, just to say hello and brighten my day. Every time the parole board denied me parole, Louise always sent me a card to uplift my spirit, encourage me to stay the course, and let me know I was in her prayers. She remained confident that my release was in the very near future. Louise's support was equal to the support I had received from Bruce and Connie, for many years. I had gained another ally.

For many years, I had been sending family members and friends gifts that I purchased from a gift catalog. The gift shop was in Arkansas, so I was ordering these gifts, via mail. I found myself sending Louise gifts I ordered from this catalog, as tokens of my appreciation of our relationship and her support. One of the gifts that Louise valued most of all, was a musical piano, made of walnut wood.

In 2001, Louise asked me what I would like to receive for a birthday gift. I told her I would like to have a pair of Lug boots. Louise sent me money to cover the cost of the boots that I wanted, and I ordered them from an institutional catalog. Most of the time, she sent me money for my birthday and Christmas. It was obvious that our relationship was evolving into more than simply a friendship. As time went on, I found myself becoming more willing to talk about sensitive and personal matters with Louise.

The time I have spent in prison, has given me the opportunity to think about countless past situations and circumstances. One night I decided to share the thoughts I was having, with Louise, so I wrote her a letter. I began by telling Louise how amazing it is that as we get older and become more mature, our perspective of past situations tends to change. I told Louise, as a kid, I was very jealous and resentful of the relationships my childhood friends shared with their grandmothers. My friend's grandmothers baked them cookies, took them shopping, and gave them all sorts of gifts. Some of my friends accompanied their grandmothers to church and often went on vacations with them. I explained I never enjoyed such relationships because my mother's mother was ill when I was a kid and she died of cancer, when I was 11 years old. I have never met my biological father, so a relationship with his mother, was not remotely possible. I then told her what I did not understand at that time, is there were grandmotherly figures living in my community who did not have grandsons and I could have formed relationships with them. They could have been my surrogate grandmothers and I could have been their surrogate grandson. When I wrote Louise this letter, I was freely sharing my feelings, without giving any thought to her reply.

Days later a letter arrived from Louise. As always, she greeted me in a warm and affectionate manner. Then Louise stated, "Terrance, sometimes you say the most profound things in your letters". She said it really touched her heart when she read what I said about not having a grandmother, and how it made me feel. Louise told me that she would be honored if from now on, I consider her to be, my "Grandma Louise".

As I glanced at the bottom of the page, I made note of her closing. It read, God bless you grandson, Grandma Louise. Imagine that! This was a life-altering moment for me. A Sicilian-Italian woman, offering to be the surrogate grandmother of an African-American man, who is serving a life sentence for murder. From that day forward this woman of Italian descent, always addressed me as grandson and I always addressed her as Grandma Louise.

Grandma Louise has a son named Sebastian, and he was very active in her everyday life. Sebastian owned and operated an Italian restaurant business for more than two decades. Daily, he went to Grandma's house to escort her to doctor appointments, visit family and friends, or anywhere else Grandma wanted to go. Sebastian did her shopping, cooking and frequently had lunch with his mother. On one of the many trips he made to her home, Grandma insisted he read a letter she had received from me.

I do not know which letter it was, but after reading my words, Sebastian told Granma, he wanted to meet me. The next time Sebastian spoke to his brother in law, Bruce, he asked Bruce, "What do I have to do to meet Terrance?" You see, Bruce Hodgin and Sebastian Bosco are brothers in laws because Bruce is married to Sebastian's sister, Connie. Bruce told Sebastian, "To visit Terrance, you must fill out and submit a visiting form to the Correctional Training Facility, where Terrance is serving time". The next time I spoke with Bruce, he told me to send him a visiting form because Connie's brother, Sebastian, would like to meet me.

Prison authorities approved Sebastian's visiting request form rather quickly, and Bruce informed me Sebastian would accompany him at our next visit. It was a Saturday morning when Bruce and Sebastian visited me the very first time. For years, Bruce, Connie and I have greeted each other with hugs, at the outset and ending of our visits. As usual, when Bruce and Sebastian entered the visiting room, I embraced Bruce with a hug. Afterwards, I extended my arm and attempted to greet Sebastian with a handshake. With a rambunctious grin on his face, Sebastian said, "No, I do not want a handshake, I also want a hug". With a high-spirited smile on my face, I greeted Sebastian with the same warm and energetic hug I had given Bruce. The warmth and energy of the hug between Sebastian and I, categorizes the friendship we have shared, throughout the years.

During the visit, Sebastian told me when he read my letter, he knew he had to meet me. He said he could sense the sincerity of my words and they moved him. He went on to say that over the years Connie and Bruce mentioned me, quite often. Talking about my educational/vocational achievements and the various activities I have participated and completed over the years. More importantly, he said they often spoke of the gains I have made in terms of understanding my past behavior and the work I have done to become a better person. Sebastian said he never thought much of it when they would mention me.

Furthermore, Sebastian said he never had any intentions of getting involved with me and he was not the sort of person who would visit someone in prison. Who could have or would have believed that words written to Grandma Louise would be the catalyst that made it possible for me to meet and befriend her son, Sebastian. I was truly beginning to understand the adage, "The pen is mightier than the sword."

Now I was corresponding with Sebastian on a regular basis, and he visited me from time to time. Sometimes he came alone, other times he came with Bruce, and on other occasions, him, Connie and Bruce came together. It was clear early on that there was a connection between Sebastian and me. Face to face discussions and the conversations we had via mail and telephone flowed freely. It was as if we had known one another for years. Mutual trust enabled us to engage in an in-depth manner without holding anything back. Once again, I found myself forming a meaningful relationship with another member of Bruce's family.

A month or so later, I received an unexpected visit from Sebastian. When I arrived in the visiting room, we embraced, purchased a few food items and sat down at our assigned table. Sebastian said he woke up that morning with intentions of spending the day with me. Of course, I was pleased he had such a revelation. A visit from friends presents an opportunity to escape the prison environment for several hours. Minutes into our initial conversation, Sebastian said, "So you sent "Grandma" a photo of yourself?" It is funny how he would call his mother Grandma, whenever he was speaking with me. I replied, "Yes, I sent her the photo last week. Since she has never met me, I thought it was appropriate that I send her a photo. Now she is familiar with her "grandson's" appearance".

We laughed for a while and then he asked the question, "Where do you think Grandma placed your picture?" I thought about the question, paused momentarily, and replied, "In the living room or in her bedroom on a piece of furniture. While laughing, Sebastian said, "No, you are not even close". He then revealed that Grandma has an industrial size refrigerator in her kitchen and photos of their family tree are on the front of her refrigerator. Every family member's photograph is on the front of Grandma's refrigerator, in the formation of a circle. Sebastian said, what photo do you believe is dead center of the circle? Before I could answer his question, Sebastian said, "You are at the center of the circle, of our family tree". He said, it is funny when family and friends see your photograph on her refrigerator for the first time. They always ask Grandma, "Louise who is that at the center of the circle". In a nonchalant manner, Grandma always replies, "Oh, that is my grandson, Terrance". Sebastian said, you should see the looks on some of their faces when she tells them you are her grandson.

I did not know it at the time, but Sebastian's wife Victoria was astonished that Sebastian quite often returned from a visit with me, in a better mood than he was in, prior to his trip to the prison. She could not understand how a trip to a prison could improve his mood or state of mind.

In September of 2001, Sebastian and his wife, Victoria went to Hawaii to celebrate their 28th wedding anniversary, in Kona, Hawaii. As a matter of fact, they were in Hawaii when the tragic 9-11 incident occurred. Since airport operations had come to a standstill, they were unable to get a flight home, so they remained in Hawaii several days beyond their intended departure.

While they were on the beach, Victoria decided to send me particles of sand from the beach and a seashell, enclosed in a plastic bag. She also sent me a post card telling me she thought she would send me a part of Kona, Hawaii. Prison officials, to my surprise, gave me the bag of sand she sent me. Unfortunately, staff did not give me the seashell. To this day, I still have every particle of sand Victoria sent me, and the sand remains in the very same plastic bag, in which she placed it.

The sand and post card represented my initial contact with Victoria. Her gesture moved and inspired me to write her a letter that she would not receive until her return from Hawaii. I thanked her for being so thoughtful and expressed the emotions I felt when I received the sand and post card, and notification, she had also enclosed a sea shell. Evidently, I said so much more, because the letter was 8 pages (front and back) in length.

Days following hers and Sebastian's return from Kona, Hawaii, I received a letter from Victoria. Her letter began with the following statement. "I cannot believe you wrote me an eight-page letter, after receiving my small post card. This would prove to be the beginning of communication in the form of letters and phone conversations, between Victoria and me. After writing and speaking with Victoria, via telephone, a few times, she decided she wanted to meet me. The feeling was mutual, so I immediately forwarded her a visiting request form. Quite often when Sebastian visited me, he would bring a stack of photographs. On many occasions the collection of photographs included pictures of Victoria, pictures of Victoria and Sebastian, pictures of Victoria and her girlfriends, and pictures of Sebastian, Victoria and their mutual friends. I was very familiar with Victoria's appearance and soon I would meet her and engage in a face to face conversation.

When it comes to meeting people, I have never been one to have a sense of apprehension or anxiety, about meeting someone for the very first time. Furthermore, Victoria and I had been corresponding and talking with one another, so it was not as if we were total strangers. I felt she was a good-natured person with a beautiful personality, and my assessment of her was correct. I will always remember the first time I met Victoria because I never could have imagined a more emotional first encounter. Sebastian, Victoria and I embraced one another and then the three of us sat down. We could not have been more than five minutes into the visit, when Victoria said, "Terrance, what can we do to help you get out of prison?" She went on to say that she and her family believe I am a good person and they want to help me gain my freedom. As she was speaking, she also was crying. I glanced at Sebastian, and immediately made note of the tears rolling down his face.

Due to the sort of person I was at that time, I was doing everything within my power, not to cry, but the situation was so overwhelming that I could no longer contain my own tears. It was unbelievable to me that someone who was meeting me for the first time could have such strong convictions about my freedom. When you consider how society in general feels about criminals, particularly, those of us who have committed murder, you will understand how miraculous it was to me that Victoria reached the conclusion I was a good person. She said she would gladly write the parole board a letter indicating her, and Sebastian would support me in any and every manner upon my release from prison. Victoria also said she could "rally the troops" by having her friends submit support letters to the parole board. I indicated I appreciated the offer but declined because I only want to receive support letters from people who know and have met me. It was crystal clear to me, that I had acquired another ally and staunch supporter, who also is a member of Bruce's family.

# CHAPTER 10

## CAGE YOUR RAGE

## REACHING OUT TO PROFESSOR MICHAEL NAGLER

At my December 2002 parole suitability hearing, the parole board granted me parole. The panel determined that I no longer posed a threat to society and I had addressed my violence related issues. When the Board grants a prisoner parole, the prisoner undergoes a 120-day review process. The Departmental Review Board (DRB) has 90 days to approve, reverse or refer the parole panel's decision to an En Banc Hearing. If the DRB approves the parole board's decision, the Governor has 30 days to approve or reverse the panel's decision granting a murderer parole. The DRB approved the parole board's decision, so I now had to await the Governor's decision. Well, on May 8, 2003, I received notice from Governor Gray Davis that he elected to exercise his right to reverse the parole board's decision. Governor Davis revoked my parole date, one day prior to my release.

In January of 2004, I enrolled and participated in the "Cage Your Rage" self-help group. This was a program that addressed violence and teaches participants coping skills. David Rosskopf, LCSW, facilitated this group. The format included a combination of videos, group inter-actions, role-playing, and log keeping. The group covered topics such as Personal History, Domestic Violence, Methods of Dealing with Anger, Ways to Recognize and Avoid Anger, and Relaxation. Upon the completion of the Cage Your Rage self-help group, another prisoner, David Rosskopf and I, established the Advanced Anger Management group. This group met on a weekly basis for more than two years. The material and curriculum included Past and Present Anger, Anger and Aggression, Domestic Violence, What Makes Us Angry, How to Manage Your Anger and the Moral, Medical and Educational Models of Violence. We included the Moral, Medical and Educational Models of Violence in our curriculum, because of a relationship I established with the man who defined these viewpoints. Please allow me to explain.

In 2004, I was reading a Yoga Journal magazine article that men-tioned a book entitled, "Is There No Other Way? The Search for a Nonviolent Future". The article mentioned that Michael Nagler, a professor at Berkeley University is the author of this publication. Furthermore, the article offered additional publications written by Michael, related to nonviolence issues. I decided to write Michael and explain that I am a nonviolence advocate who currently facili-tates workshops that address violence. I am a formerly violent person who has addressed my issues that caused me to behave violently and now my plight is to get other men to stop their violence. I requested Michael send me a copy of this book as a donation because I felt his book would aid me in the facilitation of my anger and violence related workshops. In a relatively short period of time, I received a letter from Michael, commending me for my efforts to stop prison violence. As I had requested, Michael enclosed a copy of his book "Is There No Other Way? A Search for a Nonviolent Future". I utilized his material during my facilitation of Alternatives to Violence, Cage Your Rage, and Advanced Anger Management workshops.

In this award-winning publication, Michael Nagler reveals the principles by which nonviolence functions at all levels of conflict. He makes an important distinction between strategic and principled nonviolence and demonstrates how nonviolence always works in the long run, even though changes might seem bleak at the onset.

The book "Is There No Other Way? The Search for a Nonviolent Future" begins with the achievements of Mahatma Gandhi and follows the legacy of nonviolence through the struggles against Nazism in Europe, racism in America, oppression in China and Latin America, and ethnic conflicts in Africa and Bosnia. Nonviolence, he proposes, has proven its power against arms and social injustice wherever correctly understood and applied. He then explores these same principles in the context of the growing violence of American society.

Michael Nagler is a well-known American peace scholar and founder of the University of California Peace and Conflict Studies program, at Berkeley University. His approach is not only historical, but also personal. He argues, drawing upon the experience of Gandhi and other activists that the shift to nonviolence begins within the individual, through the reshaping and re-visioning of how one understands the world. He then shows how from changes in the individual, leads to changes in the larger community. Nonviolence, is therefore, much more than a form of protest.

Michael is Professor emeritus of Classics and Comparative Literature at UC, Berkeley, where he co-founded the Peace and Conflict Studies Program in which he taught the immensely popular nonviolence course, "Meditation" and a sophomore seminar called, "Why Are We Here? -Great Writing on the Meaning of Life," for fifteen years. Among other awards, he received the Jamnalal Bajaj International Award for "Promoting Gandhian Values Outside India" in 2007, joining other distinguished contributors to nonviolence as Archbishop Desmond Tutu and peace scholar and activist Johan Galtung in receiving this honor.

He is the author of *"The Nonviolence Handbook: A Guide to Practical Action "(2014)* as well as *"The Search for a Nonviolent Future"*, which received a 2002 American Book Award and has been translated into Korean, Arabic, Italian and other languages; *"Our Spiritual Crisis: Recovering Human Wisdom in a Time of Violence"*(2005);"*The Upanishads"*(with Sri Eknath Easwaran, 1987), and other books as well as many articles on peace and spirituality.

Michael has spoken for campus, religious, and other groups on peace and nonviolence for many years, especially since September 11, 2001. He has consulted for the U.S. Institute of Peace and many other organizations and is the founder and President of the board of the Metta Center for Nonviolence Education. Michael has worked on nonviolent intervention since the 1970's and served on the Interim Steering Committee of the Nonviolent Peaceforce. Michael is a student of Sri Eknath Easwaran, founder of the Blue Mountain Center of Meditation. After reading Michael's book, I wrote him a letter to discuss the material contained therein. He became a mentor and a friend, in the process. After corresponding for many years, Michael submitted the following letter to the parole board, in my behalf.

*To Whom This May Concern:*

*I am writing to support Terrance Hunter, D32398, presently in Soledad correctional facility, whose case will come before you shortly.*

*Over the years that I was teaching in the Peace and Conflict Studies Program that I founded at the University of California Berkeley, a number of inmates of correctional facilities around the country came across one or more of my books on nonviolence and wrote to me. Some of these men impressed me with their sincerity and in some cases I entered into an extend correspondence with them. Of all these men, none has impressed me more than Mr. Hunter. I admire his intelligence and thoughtfulness; you may be aware that despite the disadvantage of his position he has done everything possible to help his sister with the care of his nieces. In fact, he asked me to speak to them to help them to help her with the choices she had to make in life, which I gladly agreed to do. Whatever may have been the crime for which he was incarcerated so long ago (and it seems to have been a kind of self-defense gone wrong) there is no question in my mind that he is no longer a threat to society.*

*Terrance has been a model prisoner and has taken every step possible to prepare himself for life in society, including numerous workshops and regular participation in the Toastmasters Club as well as training in the use of computers. I see him as not only not a threat to society but a valuable contributor to it once he gains his release. In fact, he has expressed a keen interest in working with METTA, my non-profit organization, which I and the rest of the staff were very pleased to hear. His skills in speaking and his training in computer skills will make him a valuable addition. All this, of course, in addition to his lively interest in nonviolence, which is what prompted him initially to write to me. You will have the details of his record before you, so I do not rehearse them here. I only want to repeat that in my professional and personal judgement Terrance Hunter poses no threat to society. He will, on the contrary, be a valuable member of it when he has gained his freedom. That has been the opinion also of a number of his acquaintances and of professional staff who came in contact with him during his years at Soledad.*

*I hope that these considerations will be of help to you in reaching your decision. Please do not hesitate to let me know if I can be of further help in gaining Mr. Hunter's release.*

*Sincerely yours,*
*Michael N. Nagler*
*(prof. emer.)*

On November 20, 2002, the Technology Training Foundation of America, conducted and sponsored the Computer Give Away Project. This event took place at Edward Kemble Elementary School, in Sacramento, California. During this event, K-12 schools received 1500 computer systems, and fellow technicians and I contributed 450 of those computer systems. Unfortunately, the Computer Refurbishing program ended in 2004 because some of the prisoners assigned to the shop were involved in illegal activities. As a result of their actions, many children did not experience the benefit of receiving computers systems from us, and countless prisoners did not have the opportunity to acquire gainful employment skills. Following the discontinuation of the Computer Refurbishing program, I acquired a job in the lunch box section of the culinary department.

The lunch box crew consisted of approximately 20 workers, including myself. We prepared daily lunches for the North, South, Central and East Dorm facilities, located on the CTF compound. Therefore, we prepared 7,200 lunches within a two-hour period, every day. We also performed additional culinary duties. I reported to my work assignment at 6:00 am and the day ended at about 1:30.

Upon the completion of my work assignment, on Mondays, I co-facilitated the Advanced Anger Management session. One of my co-workers on the lunch box crew was a man named Dennis Chan. However, on the main line, everyone called him "Dragon". The name was appropriate because he is a martial arts specialist. Dennis began studying martial arts when he was six years old. Every day at work, Dennis would train in the back of the culinary department. I was amazed at his conditioning and the physical feats he had mastered. For example, in a certain area of the kitchen was a steel pole that was probably 14-16 inches in diameter. Dennis would strike this pole with his shins an infinite amount of times, every morning. His shins were calloused in the same manner as one develops callouses on ones' knuckles.

Dennis and I hit it off from the very beginning. Though I am probably 10 to 15 years older than him, we developed a meaningful friendship. Our personalities were similar in many ways, and we had daily conversations that covered everything under the sun. Frequently, we talked about personal and family matters. While in many cases relationships in prison have everything to do with race and one's ethnicity, Dennis and I did not allow prison politics to interfere or hinder our friendship. Dennis quite often revealed information about his family. For instance, he shared information regarding his sister's occupation and scholastic achievements. He told me a great deal about his parents and other relatives in China. On several occasions, he shared various aspects of his childhood and Chinese traditions. I would do the same, so we reached a point in which we knew one another very well.

Dennis was serving time because when he came to America, at an early age, he was fascinated with the lifestyles led by gangsters in San Francisco's China Town. Eventually, he became an enforcer who collected debts for the mob. One of his debt collection encounters, led to him and his two co-defendants, receiving term-to-life sentences.

Though Dennis was a highly skilled martial artist, he was a mild-mannered, well disciplined and humble man. In other words, he was anything other than a bully. Quite often cell mates and prisoners on the mainline would misinterpret his kind and gentle nature, as a sign of weakness. When such occasions would arise, Dennis would re-introduce himself to such individuals, and they would incur Dragon's wrath. In some instances, correctional staff caught Dragon in the act, and his assaults led to disciplinary reports and solitary confinement.

One morning after the Lunch Box crew had finished our duties, I brought it to Dennis's attention that I facilitated an Advanced Anger Management group on Mondays. I provided a little background information about the group and gave him a pretty good idea of our agenda. Afterwards, I told him it would please me if he came to my next group meeting, as a guest. I explained that if he agreed to attend the group, he does not have to participate, join or come at any other time. Dennis agreed and stated, "He would be honored to attend".

The following Monday, Dennis and I left our work area and headed to the Advanced Anger Management group. After I had greeted the group, I announced we had a guest and I asked him to introduce himself to the group. Most of the men in the room were already familiar with Dennis. I advised Dennis it is his option to participate in the various discussions and topics we will cover, or not to do so. It is totally up to him.

In the Advance Anger Management group, participants can bring a situation they encountered, a close encounter or any other potentially volatile situation to the group's attention. Participants may bring an issue to the group's attention, to seek solutions that may avoid a confrontation. As the facilitator, I can bring a subject matter to the group and the floor is also open for participants to do the same. As the group progressed, Dennis became more actively involved in our group discussions. It was obvious to me he was becoming more comfortable with the group and the material covered. At the conclusion of the group, we always give guest an opportunity to assess the group and give an account of their experience. Dennis indicated he didn't know what to expect when I invited him to the group and he was glad that he came. He said he enjoyed the topics we covered, and he wanted to come back. The next week when Dennis arrived, he brought pork, beef and chicken burritos that he made personally, for the entire group.

It must have been a few weeks following Dennis's first time attending the Advanced Anger Management group. He came into the Lunch Box room and it was obvious to me that he was upset. Without greeting me, Dennis said, "T, I need to talk to you?" I started walking towards the back of the culinary department, where he and I could talk privately. When we reached a point in which we were beyond the range of listening ears, I stopped and asked Dennis, "What happened?" Dennis explained that the day before he was on the recreation yard playing handball with another prisoner, and the dude started "Talking shit". Dennis said, "I wanted to break his face, I wanted to kick his ass". Then he told me, "But I did not do anything because I thought about what you have been teaching me in the Advanced Anger Management group. What you said about how we give our power away when we let someone upset us. What you said about how easy it is to strike someone when they piss you off, but more difficult to walk away. How you explained that we let our pride and ego stop us from making good decisions. For those reasons, I just walked away from the handball court."

At that moment, I was so proud of Dennis and I told him so. The point is, he is more than capable of breaking that guy's face and kicking his ass, but he didn't. It was important that I reinforced the message that he had done the right thing and his failure to act did not make him less of a man, but more of a man. I let him know he had conducted himself responsibly and for that he should be proud of himself.

I further reiterated how disappointed his family would have been if he had assaulted the other guy, and what that would have meant at his upcoming parole hearing. At the conclusion of my affirmations, Dennis turned to me and said, "T, I cannot even talk to my own people (Chinese prisoners) about situations like this. He told me he really values our friendship and the knowledge he has gained since attending the Advanced Anger Management group.

At Dennis's next parole board hearing, the parole board found him suitable for parole. After the hearing, he informed me, for the first time since he began going before the parole board, he was able to answer their questions about his violence. He said he felt comfortable talking about and explaining his anger and violent behavior and at the conclusion of the hearing, the panel commended him for the work he had done to address his violence. Dennis told me he informed the panel he had learned what he learned from his friend, "T". To prove what he had told me, he allowed me to read his parole board transcripts, and he did in fact, attribute his gainful insight to what he learned in my group. Dennis told me he will always be grateful of the time I spent helping him gain control of his emotions and behavior. Upon Dennis's release from prison, authorities deported him to China, even though the members of his immediate family all live here in the United States.

# CHAPTER 11

## AVP COMES TO THE CTF
## THE MEANING OF A GRIEVANCE STORY

In March of 2006, the institution's closed-circuit television system broadcasted a notice that the warden wanted to bring the Alternatives to Violence Project, to CTF. Ms. Jackie Kramer, the Associate Warden's secretary, requested that any AVP facilitator who is interested in facilitating AVP workshops, contact her office. In response to Ms. Kramer's announcement, eight AVP facilitators responded and indicated we were interested in helping get this program underway. We met in the Associates Warden's office to formulate a plan and become familiar with one another.

The Santa Cruz/Salinas Valley AVP Counsel, was sponsoring The AVP program coming to CTF. Initially, I had contact with whom I consider the core members of the AVP Santa Cruz/Salinas Valley Counsel. Individuals such as George Ramos, Mimi Edgar, Alan Edgar, John Devalcourt, Betty Devalcourt, Robin Keeler, Terrill Keeler, and Linda McCue. To conduct an AVP workshop, at least one outside community volunteer must be present. This policy is due to the necessity of having someone in the room that is in possession of an alarm they can activate, if a volatile situation or an emergency arises. Without the help of these dedicated volunteers, establishing AVP at CTF would not have been possible.

Bringing AVP to CTF posed a challenge that did not exist at San Quentin. When I participated in AVP at San Quentin, the bad relations that existed between African American and Southern Mexican prisoners, was not an issue because there were no Southern Mexicans on the mainline. There were only Northern Mexican prisoners on the mainline at San Quentin. Conducting workshops that included Northern Mexicans was not a problem. African Americans and Northern Mexicans have always had a cooperative relationship, during my period of incarceration. At certain institutions, we were actual allies. However, there was bad blood between Southern Mexican and African American prisoners at CTF, and many if not most of the melees that took place at CTF, at one point, involved Southern Mexicans and African Americans.

I can recall the first workshop I facilitated. You must understand one thing about AVP workshops. Every workshop is racially balanced. There are an equal number of prisoners representing every race. In other words, the workshop included five (5) African Americans, five (5) Caucasian, five (5) Asian and five (5) Hispanic prisoners. So, for the first time, I was facilitating a workshop that included Southern Mexicans and African Americans. In AVP workshops, participants must interact in an up-close-and personal manner. It was going to be interesting to see if individuals who would have absolutely nothing to do with each other on a day to day basis, would interact with each other in the workshop.

On the first day of a three-day workshop, the team of AVP facilitators attempt to create an atmosphere that will enable participants to feel comfortable enough to talk about personal and sensitive matters.

We begin by introducing ourselves to the group. I generally tell participants I have been involved in AVP since 1995, and I continue to facilitate AVP workshops because of the impact AVP has had in my life and I believe in the work we do. I inform the group AVP is an experiential workshop and what you get out of the experience depends upon the effort you put forth. We tell participants the group is a community and we'll try to build enough trust in one another to feel safe and secure together. We request their help to bring this about, by observing and following certain agreements.

One of the most important observed agreements, is confidentiality, regarding the personal sharing of each participant. This is an agreement that participants will not repeat anything said in the workshop, that is personal, outside the workshop. In other words, we agree to not to repeat anything said in the workshop, to anyone in the general population.

There was a Southern Mexican in this workshop, named Tony, who was a "shot caller". In other words, he had major influence on the Southern Mexican population. On the first day, Tony's participation increased as the workshop progressed. On the second day, Tony approached me during one of the breaks and said, "T, you are OK with me man, because you are "keeping it real". He made the statement I am keeping it real, because in AVP workshops I do not pull any punches, or sugar coat anything. Quite often I say things and take positions that are not popular. Tony then said, "When I see you on the mainline, we are going to kick-it". Both statements were unbelievable when one understands the lack of communication/conversation that generally takes place between African-American and Southern Mexican prisoners. When Tony made those statements, I did not take them to heart or expect him to follow through. I felt he was "caught up" in the moment and the atmosphere of the workshop. Comparable to what takes place during prison Sunday morning church services. It is common for prisoners of different races to embrace one another during a Sunday morning service, only to walk past one another like total strangers, on the recreation yard in the afternoon. This is due to the racial divide that exists in the California Prison System.

What is so amazing about an AVP workshop is the atmosphere and the exercises we perform can stir the emotions of the most hardened criminal. It is common for men who have not shed a tear in years to find themselves crying profusely, when an exercise, discussion or some other event triggers an emotion that he cannot control. Quite often this occurs when a participant talks about his family or some past traumatic event. At other times, prisoners feel such emotions, when he comes to the realization of the harm, pain and suffering that he has inflicted upon those whom he has victimized.

The workshop was a success and the interaction that took place between African American and Southern Mexicans reinforced my belief in the program. The true test would be determined by whether the interaction between the two groups would continue after the workshop ended. Whether participants would continue to engage in the same manner on the mainline, or cave in to peer pressure. It must have been a couple days following the workshop that I saw Tony, the Southern Mexican shot caller, for the first time. He was at the East Gate with three of his soldiers. When he saw me, he said, "Hey, what's up, T?" He approached me, and we shook hands and embraced. The East Gate is a location where there is always a congregation or group of 10 or more prisoners. There were numerous African Americans and Southern Mexicans observing the interaction between Tony and me, including the three guys who were with Tony. None of them or anyone else said anything. When Tony and I concluded our conversation, we shook hands, embraced and said we would see each other later.

As I watched Tony and his amigos depart, I noticed they were talking to him as they walked away. There is no doubt in my mind they asked him, "What's up with that dude?" I'm certain they discussed me because the next time I came across Tony and the same three guys, all three of them said, "What's up T?" Apparently, Tony told them I was cool.

One of the reasons Tony said that I was keeping it real in the workshop is because I made a statement regarding individuals such as him, who have influence and control of a certain segment of the population. I made him aware of the fact, he has the power to influence his people to commit criminal acts. I told him the very same power can influence the same people, in a positive manner.

As we conducted more AVP workshops and the percentage of the population of AVPers increased, a noticeable change was taking place. As more African American and Southern Mexicans participated in AVP workshops, we discovered what we have in common far outweigh our differences. We discovered we share common interest when it comes to family matters and in many instances, we share similar life experiences. In AVP we have exercises that require us to look into one another's eyes as we answer a question, recount an incident or perform some other act. In most cases, this is the first-time participants have looked into the eyes of a person they are speaking or listening to. There are exercises in which we are the speaker and at other times, the listener. Though we talk about violence and the root causes of violence, we do not spend very much time on this subject. Most of the time, we are engaged in activities that enable participants to gain communication and social skills, unconsciously.

The culture at CTF changed before my very eyes, and it was due to the fact, AVP had come to CTF. Suddenly, we found ourselves playing sports, working with and living in the same housing units, as our AVP brothers. At the end of an AVP workshop, participants receive an AVP pin that they wear on their shirt collar/pocket, jacket, or any other area of their clothing. In wearing our AVP pin, it identifies us with other graduates of AVP. It is common for AVP graduates to strike-up a conversation with a stranger, who is wearing an AVP pin. We took the concept that we are a community to heart, and it changed the atmosphere at CTF from a very hostile to a more cooperative environment.

When a participant completes an AVP Basic workshop, he can request to have his name placed on the waiting list for the Advanced AVP workshop. After completing the Advanced AVP workshop, he can then request to have his name placed on the waiting list for the Training for Trainers workshop. Completion of this workshop entitles graduates to facilitate AVP workshops. Eventually, many of the Southern Mexicans who participated in AVP workshops, made the transition from participant to facilitator. At CTF we established weekly Mini AVP workshops as a support group for AVP alumni.

The Mini workshop at CTF is unique and does not exist at any other prison. My fellow AVP facilitators and I thought this would be a good vehicle that would allow us to strengthen our bond with fellow AVPers and break the cycle of prisoners using race to determine their viewpoint of fellow prisoners. After facilitating the first AVP workshop at CTF, I received the document below, from Associate Warder J.C. Sisk.

> *Mr. Hunter voluntarily contributed 21 hours of his time, during a two-day period, as a facilitator for the Alternatives to Violence Project (AVP) Basic Workshop, conducted on August 21 & 22, 2006. The AVP Program is an internationally recognized program designed to empower people to lead non-violent lives through affirmation, respect for all, community building, cooperation and trust.*

*Mr. Hunter first attended his Basic AVP Workshop in California State Prison at San Quentin (March 29, 30, 31, 1995) and his Advanced AVP Workshop in California State Prison at San Quentin (May 3, 4, 5, 1995). Mr. Hunter became eligible to attend the Training for Trainers AVP Workshop and did so in California State Prison at San Quentin (June 20, 21, 22, 1995). After successfully completing training and certification by AVP/USA, Mr. Hunter was authorized to conduct AVP Basic, Advanced and Training for Trainers workshops, in conjunction with national and international facilitators. During the AVP Basic Workshop conducted on August 21 & 22, 2006, Mr. Hunter worked with local civilian AVP facilitators and inmate facilitators by providing support and facilitating the learning process of the participants. Workshop elements included principles of cooperation with coworkers, developing listening skills, promoting communication skills, and developing tools for stress and anger management. The intent of the workshop is to develop comprehensive alternatives to violent situations involving non-violent solutions, which reflect a caring attitude towards each individual participant and others.*

*On July 19, 2006, Mr. George Ramos (Regional AVP Liaison to CTF) personally interviewed Mr. Hunter to ascertain the validity of his AVP certification. Mr. Ramos chose Mr. Hunter as an inmate facilitator for one of the first AVP workshops at CTF Central, conducted on August 21 & 22, 2006. Mr. Hunter is to be commended for successfully facilitating the AVP Workshop and his individual contribution*

*to promoting a peaceful, non-violent programming environ-
ment at the Correctional Training Facility.*

*J.C. Sisk*
*Associate Warden*
*CTF-Central Facility*
*02/23/2007*

In early July of 2006, I greeted a staff member whom I had spoken to many times in route to my culinary work assignment. I assumed he worked in the Infirmary because he always appeared to be coming or going in that direction. On this morning, he introduced himself as, Dr. Ira Katz and then asked me my name. Dr. Katz told me he had made note of my upbeat character whenever he has encountered me in the hallway and asked if I would be interested in an upcoming program that he would be facilitating; the "Forgiveness for Health, Happiness and Conflict Resolution Group." Following his brief description of the program, I gave him my CDC identification number and told him to sign me up.

Dr. Katz's Forgiveness for Health, Happiness and Conflict Resolution Group, was a twenty (20) week program. The program focused on learning new skills, and/or improving previously learned skills, such as victim awareness, forgiveness training practices, conflict resolution, anger management, peaceful settlements, stress management, increasing self-awareness, and personal growth. In this group, each participant wrote, expressed and resolved our own "grievance story".

Furthermore, participants made a commitment to changing negative experience stories to positive intention stories and practicing "Positive Emotion Refocusing Technique" (PERT) and the HEAL method "Hope-Educate-Affirm-Long-term) commitment.

Participation in Dr. Katz program proved to be an eye-opening experience and one of the many turning points I experienced during my period of confinement. Dr. Katz introduced me to what is known as a "grievance story." Though I had never heard the term, when Dr. Katz explained its meaning, I immediately identified with the behavior associated with the term. A grievance story is a story told from a victim's perspective and it is a story told repeatedly. Usually, many aspects of the story are not true or may be partially true. The thing about a grievance story is the more you tell the story, the more realistic the story becomes to the person telling the story.

On countless occasions, I told the story, my stepfather forced me to leave home at the age of 15 because I had a turbulent relationship with him. However, by participating in Dr. Katz's program, I realized the story I have told is not true. The following is an accurate account of what happened.

One day while my mother and stepfather were at work, I placed a lock on my bedroom door. I was 15 years old at the time, and I placed the lock on my door, so my younger siblings could not enter my room when I was not at home. That night, my stepfather came to my room to talk to me about a chore. Since I locked the door, he had to knock on the door. When I opened the door, he saw the lock, grabbed a hammer and beat the lock until the lock fell to the floor. He then asked me why I had placed a lock on the door without permission to do so. Though I did not verbalize my sentiments, I was thinking I did not need permission, since taking care of my younger siblings were adult-like responsibilities. Instead of answering my stepfather's question, in anger, I stated I was moving away from home.

The truth of the matter is, over the years I portrayed my stepfather as someone who beat the lock like a mad man. I even implied he made threatening gestures while holding the hammer in his hand, but that also is not true. My stepfather was a good man, and an ideal male role model. His mother and father died when he was very young and at the age of 15, he joined the U.S. Army by falsely stating his age to the recruiter.

My stepfather is a veteran of the Korean War. When he was 17 years old the Koreans captured him and for the next five years, his captors severely tortured him. The Army was unaware of his POW status, so they informed his family he was dead. The Koreans released him when he was 22 years old and he then returned to the United States. For five years, the Koreans fed my stepfather nothing other than sea weed, so his digestive system was devastated. Despite his misfortunes in life, my stepfather was a mild-mannered man, who provided for our family. Though he had every cause to be resentful and bitter, he was always very respectful towards me, my mother and siblings. Unfortunately, I never had the opportunity to tell my stepfather how I feel about him today because in 1985 he passed away, after suffering an asthma/heart attack. To make amends, in a letter to my mother, I apologized for my past distorted/slanted viewpoints of my stepfather. It would have been great having a man to man conversation with him, today, and I am certain he would be pleased with the man I have become.

When I decided to leave home, I was not angry about anything my stepfather said or did that night. I was angry because my stepfather forced me to quit playing baseball at the local park, basketball at school, and athletics at the YMCA, to baby sit my younger siblings. My mother's work schedule changed and instead of getting home at 3:00 pm she was now getting home at 11:00 pm. As the oldest of my parent's siblings still living at home, it became my job to care for my siblings. Though I loved my siblings dearly, I did not like sacrificing something in which I enjoyed doing. That was the true source of my anger and my motivation for moving away from home that night and abandoning my family. I had not yet learned the concept of "fight or flight" but that night I felt I did not stand up to my stepfather. I can vividly remember telling myself, that night, that I am not going to take any shit from anyone ever again. That position taken at the age of 15, would prove to be one of the causes of my downfall, many years later.

Through my exploration of the anger I felt when I had to stop playing sports, I have gained a better understanding of why I was so upset. When I began playing baseball at the local ballpark, I was a pitcher, first baseman and I played center field. I was a good ball player and frequently my skills enabled me to help my team win games. My coaches, team mates, and their families cheered for me and showered me with accolades regarding my performance. I felt like I was a part of a very large family and this family valued and appreciated me. Though my parents never came to a single practice or game, my coaches and my team mate's parents took care of me when I was at the park. It was as if I had five or six dads helping me with my fielding, batting and pitching. Furthermore, someone always bought me refreshments and offered me a ride home after games and practices. I was one of three African American kids on the team and our race did not matter. My team mates and their parents did not concern themselves with the color of my skin and I can honestly say I never experienced any form of racism at the ballpark. I felt special when I was playing baseball and during this time in my life, I felt good about myself. The day I went to the field to turn in my uniform, I can recall the guilt I felt. My team depended on me and by quitting the team, in my mind I let down my coaches and team mates.

My anger caused me to move away from home, abandoning my family when they needed me. I also severed ties with my relatives because I have not attended our yearly family reunions, since I was 15 years old. That would prove to be one of the worst decisions I have ever made in life and the beginning of countless poor decisions. I will forever be grateful of meeting Dr. Katz and the insight I gained from his Forgiveness for Health, Happiness and Conflict Resolution Group. It was during my participation in his group that I realized I had been telling a story and viewing myself as a victim. My relationship with Dr. Katz went beyond the twenty-week period of the group. I would later become his assistant and co-facilitator in his Forgiveness for Health, Happiness and Conflict Resolution Group and his Life Skills for Lifers group. In acknowledgment of my contributions, Dr. Katz issued me the following documents.

*April 27, 2007*

*This Laudatory Chrono is to commend Inmate Hunter, for taking an active role in the development of the "Life Skills for Lifers" group. Mr. Hunter also volunteered and was trained to be a co-facilitator of one of our six groups of four. He has co-facilitated this weekly 90-minute group for the past three months.*

*Terrance Hunter has demonstrated a commitment to learning and recovery excellence by providing education to other inmate learners. Mr. Hunter is a very committed and dedicated facilitator. He has read all educational materials provided to him and has referred multiple other inmates to the group. He has also shared his experiences with the peaceful settlements program of Dr. Michael Nagler of the University of California, Berkeley. These research concepts have enriched our class.*

*This is an example of his demonstrable initiative in the development of group topics and in tailoring our educational materials to the real-time life experiences of fellow inmates. Inmate Hunter makes a clear effort to reach out to group members of all races and has provided continued support, wisdom, and encouragement to group members both inside and outside of the group setting. It has been a pleasure to work with Mr. Hunter and I am encouraged that he will continue to make a positive impact to those around him.*

*Ira Katz, PhD*
*Clinical Psychologist*
*Correctional Training Facility, Soledad*

*July 11, 2007*

*This Laudatory Chrono is to commend Inmate Hunter for taking a leadership role as a Co-Facilitator in the development and delivery of the "Life Skills for Lifers" group. This large group (24 participants) that meets for 20 weeks/50 hours, with the focus on bringing Cognitive behavioral therapy skills into the lives of inmates serving life terms would not have been possible without the individual and team effort of Mr. Hunter.*

*The program took a great deal of planning and thought before being implemented in March 2007. There were 6 Co-Facilitators selected and trained by materials Dr. Katz utilized from the American Community Corrections Institute. Inmate Hunter was given Facilitator Training materials to learn and apply the principles in our group. Inmate Hunter attended the monthly facilitator meeting to help fine tune the on-going group. Inmate Hunter's feedback was instrumental in making the group experience even better.*

*Within his own group, Inmate Hunter has modeled what he has learned. Mr. Hunter's role as Co-Facilitator has benefited us all. I am grateful for Inmate Hunter's willingness to serve and help others.*

*Katz, PhD*
*Staff Psychologist*
*CTF Soledad*

# CHAPTER 12

## MICROSOFT OFFICE CERTIFICATION
## TOASTMASTERS INTERNATIONAL

In December of 2006, I learned there were plans to introduce anoth-er vocational trade to the mainline at CTF. According to rumors, the Office Services and Related Technologies (OSRT) vocational trade would be open by the end of the month. I contacted my counselor to inquire about the rumor and discovered it was true. I had been working in the Lunch Box room ever since the Computer Refurbishing pro-gram closed, so I immediately requested an assignment in the OSRT vocational trade. The OSRT vocational trade would include a combi-nation of user-end computer skills and training associated with admin-istrative office duties.

When I reported to the OSRT classroom, I immediately realized I was looking at the very same antiquated computer systems and soft-ware, that I utilized in the Data Processing vocational trade, more than 10 years ago. The instructor was a woman, and I approached her to inquired about the arrival date of our new computers and software. She replied, "What new computers and software? These are the computer systems that we will be utilizing in the program." I told her she should contact the principle and request more up-to-date systems and software. She advised me she had already requested new systems from the principle, and he stated she would not receive new computers and the issue is not open for discussion. I then asked her what she said when he told her the issue is not open for discussion. She said she did not say anything because he is her boss and she did not want to upset him. I advised her he is not my boss and this issue is far from closed. I told her I would resolve the issue by filing an appeal.

Any prisoner under the California Department of Corrections and Rehabilitation's jurisdiction, may appeal any policy, decision, action, condition, or omission by the department or its staff that the prisoner can demonstrate as having a material adverse effect upon his or her health, safety, or welfare. To file an appeal, prisoners must utilize the CCDCR form #602.

That day, at lunch time, I returned to my housing unit and obtained a CDCR form #602. In my appeal I indicated, Governor Arnold Schwarzenegger had recently allocated millions of dollars to the CDCR and that money was allocated for academic and vocational programs. In my complaint I indicated staff at CTF recently activated the OSRT vocational program and the classroom is equipped with the outdated and antiquated computer systems and software that was utilized in the Data Processing program that existed in the early 1990's. The idea behind the funding provided by Governor Schwarzenegger was to enable CDCR to provide training/skills for prisoners that would allow us to compete in the job market upon our release. It is ludicrous to launch a vocational program in December 2006, utilizing 1990 technology, and expect prisoners to compete with individuals who have up-to-date computer skills. Furthermore, in my appeal I exposed the practice of misappropriating funds that has been taking place at CTF since the day I arrived at that institution. In the "Action requested" area of the appeal, I stated I request the OSRT classroom receive new systems and software, utilizing the money CTF received from Governor Schwarzenegger. I further requested that prisoners assigned to the OSRT program be permitted to take the same MOS (Microsoft Office Specialist) certification exams that students at universities take, after completing the same material our curriculum covers.

The next day, when I returned to my job assignment, I allowed the instructor to read my appeal. After reading its content, she said, "You are going to submit this appeal?" I said, "Of course, I am." Later that day, my instructor had lunch with the principal's secretary. During lunch, the principal's secretary asked my instructor if she was aware of the fact, that one of her students filed an appeal against the program. My instructor denied being aware of the appeal.

When my instructor returned from lunch, she requested I come to her desk because she wanted to tell me something. According to her, the principal's secretary said the principal and the Vocational Superintendent, were trying to determine their response to my appeal. I told her, I'm certain they are contemplating their response because they do not want my appeal to leave this institution. If my appeal leaves the institution, authorities in Sacramento will learn they are not utilizing the funding they received for its intended purpose.

An hour later, the Vocational Superintendent, came to the OSRT classroom. After he had briefly spoken with my instructor, she said, "Mr. Hunter, the Vocational Superintendent would like to speak with you." As I approached him, he extended his arm and shook my hand, as he introduced himself. He asked me to step out to the hallway, so he could have a word with me. When we had exited the classroom, he said he would like to speak with me, regarding the appeal I had filed. At that point, I told him there is nothing to discuss and I have said all that I intend to say in my appeal. He attempted to say something to me, but I simply returned to my classroom and sat in the seat at my computer.

Though we were in the hallway, my instructor and classmates were able to hear what had taken place. Ms. Florence said, "Mr. Hunter, you are very bold." I replied, He is your superior, not mine. His title means absolutely nothing to me. He is just a man.

Two days later, the Vocational Superintendent returned to the OSRT classroom. Moments after his arrival, my instructor said, "Mr. Hunter, the Vocational Superintendent would like to speak with you." While seated at my computer, I said, "I have nothing to say to him." the Vocational Superintendent then stated, "I have some documents that I want you to review." At that point, I made note of the stack of documents that he was holding. When we stepped out into the hall-way, he informed me he had ordered new computers and software for the OSRT classroom and he wanted to know if I approved. As I reviewed the documentation, he had acquired from the Procurement Office, I made note of the new Gateway systems and software packages we were receiving.

I then inquired about students taking the MOS certification exams, once we have completed the curriculum. He explained a network between a testing system in the classroom, and a system in the principal's office, would accommodate my request. Via the principal's computer, certification exams would be down-loaded from Microsoft and up-loaded to the testing system in our classroom, to enable students to take the MOS exams. Once we have completed the exam, the principle would upload the test results to Microsoft. I advised the Vocational Superintendent I was pleased with the systems and software package, and I signed and terminated my appeal. When I returned to my class-room, my instructor said, "So what will we be receiving Mr. Hunter?' I provided the details to her and my classmates and everyone was ecstatic about the new systems/software we were receiving, and our access to MOS certification credentials.

Initially, when fellow prisoners learned I had enrolled in the Office Services and Related Technology vocational program, they questioned my motives since I had already completed the Data Processing vocational trade. One individual said he did not understand my decision because the class room has the same outdated systems and software that he and I utilized in the Data Processing program. Though I had intentions of filing an appeal and requesting updated systems and software, I did not reveal those intentions to anyone. My objective was to upgrade my software application skills and I was confident I would win my appeal. It has been my experience during my period of confinement that whenever I have had a legitimate grievance, and I presented a compelling argument in the form of an appeal, the authorities have granted my request.

Enrolling in the OSRT program proved to be a wise and rewarding decision in many ways. First, it afforded me the opportunity to upgrade my knowledge of Windows software, by becoming proficient in the use of Microsoft Office 2007 applications. It was a pleasure reporting to the class room each morning because it was an ideal environment for learning. Many of the men in the class were members of AVP and other self-help programs that I facilitated, so we all were familiar with one another. Most of the men in the class were serving life term sentences and had reached a point in which we were trying to utilize our time in a productive manner. I was more familiar with computers and software than anyone else in the class because I had completed the Data Processing program. When the instructor became aware of my skills, she frequently requested my assistance. It did not take very long for my fellow students to realize I can assist them, and I was more than willing to do so. I believe in the process of helping my classmates, my sense of self-worth and self-esteem increased. It was gratifying to know others valued what I had to offer.

In July of 2007, a friend approached me and asked if I would be interested in joining the Toastmasters International Club that he was in the process of establishing at CTF. He was very active in the Protestant Church and a member of the Alternatives to Violence Project. I contemplated telling him I was not interested in joining the Toastmasters Club because my plate was full, at that time. However, I had intentions of working with troubled youth and telling my life story, upon my release from prison, so I deduced public speaking skills would aid me in my efforts. The name of the Toastmasters International Club we established at CTF is, "Talk the Line."

For those of you who may not be familiar with Toastmasters International, I will provide an overview of this organization. Toastmasters began as a series of speaking clubs organized by Ralph C. Smedley during his time working for the YMCA (Young Men's Christian Association) in Bloomington, Illinois, United States. As director of education at the YMCA, Smedley saw a need for the men in the community to learn how to speak, conduct meetings, plan programs and work on committees, and he wanted to help them. Smedley decided to organize a club where they could learn these skills in a social environment, and the men responded well to the concept. He named the group the Toastmasters Club; "toastmaster" was a popular term that referred to a person who gave toasts at banquets and other occasions.

The first unofficial Toastmasters meeting took place on March 24, 1905. Much like Toastmasters meetings today, the participants took turns leading and speaking at each meeting. Smedley and the older, more experienced men evaluated short speeches, while the younger men participated in the evaluation process. However, Smedley received positions at other YMCAs in Illinois, and later, in San Jose, California. As a result of his absence, the fledgling clubs lacked leadership and did not flourish.

Smedley began working at the newly organized YMCA in Santa Ana, California, in 1922, and for the first two years, he spent his time building a home for the organization. However, his passion to help others learn to speak and lead remained. Smedley christened the new YMCA building on April of 1924, and he was able to introduce the idea of Toastmasters to his colleagues and organize the Toastmasters club that eventually became Club No. 1 of Toastmasters International. The first meeting took place at the YMCA building on October 22, 1924. Word spread about Smedley's Toastmasters clubs and soon people in surrounding communities and other states were asking how they could start their own club.

To save time replying to the many letters and inquiries he was receiving, Smedley wrote the "Manual of Instructions" and "Ten Lessons in Public Speaking," which he had printed and bound in paper covers. On October 25, 1928, he secured copyrights on the publications and trademarked the name "Toastmasters Club." By 1930, nearly 30 Toastmasters clubs had formed including a club in British Columbia, Canada. To reflect expansion outside of the United States, the newly formed association was re-named Toastmasters International. Two years later, in 1932, Toastmasters International became an incorporation, as a California non-profit organization and Smedley took on the positions of Secretary and Editor of the new association.

The following is the mission of Toastmasters International:

> *Toastmasters International is the leading movement devoted to making effective oral communication a worldwide reality. Through its member clubs, Toastmasters International helps men and women learn the art of speaking, listening and thinking – vital skills that promote self-actualization, enhance leadership potential, foster human understanding and contribute to the betterment of mankind.*

It is basic to this mission that Toastmasters International continually expand its worldwide network of clubs, thereby offering ever-greater numbers of people the opportunity to benefit from its programs.

Now I will provide the mission of every Toastmasters International club.

> *The mission of a Toastmasters International club is to pro-*
> *vide a mutually supportive and positive learning environ-*
> *ment in which every member has the opportunity to develop*
> *communication and leadership skills, which in turn foster*
> *confidence and personal growth.*

Being a Toastmaster means more than simply making a commit-ment to self-development. Everyone who joins a Toastmasters club is making a commitment to the club, to its members and to the orga-nization. The Toastmaster International Organization has more than 313,000 members in more than 14,650 clubs in 126 countries.

It was not until June 5th, 2008, that Talk the Line conducted our very first elections and I had the honor of becoming our very first club pres-ident. Below is a copy of the document prepared by our club's sponsor.

> *On June 5th, 2008, Inmate Hunter became the first elected*
> *president of the Talk the Line chapter of the international*
> *group Toastmasters. Hunter has been a founding member*
> *as well as a member with excellent attendance. Hunter was*
> *elected because he is well respected within the group and has*
> *strength of character that is demonstrated with little fuss or*
> *boasting. I find, as a member and as the club's sponsor that*
> *Hunter will make an enormous contribution as the club's*
> *president and I look forward to seeing the club go forward*
> *with his leadership.*

> *Chamberlain*
> *Teacher*
> *Correctional Training Facility*

In addition to attending our weekly club meetings, we formulated committees that hosted events that informed the general population of our organization. Some committees would attend other self-help groups and others would enter classrooms in the Education Department, to provide students information concerning Toastmasters. During such events, members of Toastmasters would present prepared speeches to demonstrate the art of public speaking. We also advised the audience of the various functionary roles we performed at weekly meetings.

One self-help group at CTF focused on the young men who were serving time at the institution. The group was known as "Life Cycle" and the objective was to provide the participants with the "life skills" needed to successfully re-enter society. On several occasions, I received invitations to speak at Life Cycle meetings to share my life experiences, with the young men who were in the program. Speaking at such events, presented opportunities to utilize skills I acquired from Toastmasters International Club meetings.

The Toastmasters International Club experience proved to be far more rewarding than simply learning the art of public speaking. Our club membership ranged from 30 to 35 members at any given time. We met on a weekly basis, and during that time we interacted with one another on an interpersonal level. To accomplish our objectives, it was imperative that we functioned in a manner that demonstrated collective cooperation and support. In the process of conducting our affairs, we were obtaining social, leadership and communication skills that were not so obvious. When you meet weekly with a group of men, bonding takes place and you establish a sense of camaraderie. While at CTF I achieved my Toastmasters Competent Communicator, Competent Leader, Advanced Communicator Bronze and Advanced Communicator Silver awards.

Toastmasters meetings take place on Thursdays and AVP mini workshops take place on Mondays. Prior to my appearance before the

Board of Parole Hearings, on April 25, 2008,' the Santa Cruz/Monterey Area AVP Council presented me the letter below, in acknowledgement of my services. This is merely one of the many support letters submitted in my behalf.

> *This is to commend Terrance Hunter for his participation as an inmate facilitator for the Alternatives to Violence Project workshops in the Central Facility of the Correctional Training Facility in Soledad, California. AVP is an all-volunteer organization which was begun in the 1970's as collaboration between prison inmates and Quakers in New York State. Mr. Hunter has contributed immensely to the success of the AVP training in Central with his hard work, regular attendance and behavior that exemplifies the mission of AVP. He has worked collaboratively with both inside and outside facilitators to make our workshops run smoothly and has been instrumental in training more than 10% of the population of Central in ways of avoiding violence and creating a positive community.*
>
> *AVP facilitators must act as instructors, introducing and leading exercises in communication, listening, finding alternatives to old behavior patterns, and resolving conflict. This must be done in a way that opens the hearts and minds of the participants to new ways of looking at the world and relationships. This takes considerable training, skill, practice and commitment to the goals of AVP.*
>
> *The facilitators refine their own individual ability to respond to potentially conflictual or confrontational situations in a non-violent manner as they work to train others. The facilitation requires compassion toward their fellow inmates.*

*Mr. Hunter has demonstrated all of the above skills and attributes in the time since we implemented this program in Central Facility in early 2006. There are three levels of 22-hour workshops – Basic, Advanced and Training for Facilitators. Few facilitators have participated in more workshops than Mr. Hunter, who has facilitated in six 22-hour workshops and 33 follow-up mini workshops. He is an outstanding facilitator. He is articulate, sensitive and caring, with a serene, wise presence, which helps participants take the exercise seriously and urges them to look within themselves and find their own wisdom.*

*Sincerely,*
*The outside facilitators of the*
*Santa Cruz/Monterey Area AVP Council*

Unfortunately, despite the many positive letters submitted by my supporters, the gains I had made throughout the years, and psychological evaluations stating I did not pose a threat to society and was suitable for parole, the Parole Board found me to be unsuitable for parole and gave me a three-year denial.

# CHAPTER 13

## TRANSFORMING POWER

O n 2/19/2009, I obtained my Microsoft Certified Application Specialist certificate for Excel and PowerPoint. On 5/25/2009, I obtained the same certification for Microsoft Office Word and on 6/25/2009, I achieved the same certification for Microsoft Office Access. For the record, my certificates are official certification documents from Microsoft. All four of my certifications have Steven A. Ballmer's signature. He is the Chief Executive Officer, of Microsoft Corporation. Upon graduating from the OSRT vocational program, my instructor hired me as her Teacher's Aide. Providing Microsoft Office 2007 assistance to students enrolled in the vocational program and aiding them in their preparation for Microsoft Office Specialist certification exams, were my primary responsibilities. Below, is the document prepared by Ms. Florence when I became her Teacher's Aide.

*Inmate Hunter was assigned to the Teacher's Aide position, TEA%C.032 for the Office Services and Related Technologies program on March 5, 2010, one day following his successful completion of the program, as a student. Due to Inmate Hunter's highly proficient computer, technical and communication skills, he was selected for this position.*

*In the Teacher's Aide capacity, Inmate Hunter assists in preparing the students for the official Microsoft Office Specialist certification exams through one-on-one tutoring, whole class demonstrations, and hands-on-training. Inmate Hunter makes himself available to answer questions and helps to create a positive learning environment. In addition to his Teacher's Aide duties, Inmate Hunter has also contributed to the success of the annual vocational graduation ceremony for the past two years. In doing so, he personally designed the graduation brochures and invitations for the event. Moreover, Inmate Hunter served as the greeter at the ceremony, and demonstrated his friendly and courteous nature to each guest as they entered the facility's visiting room.*

*Mrs. G. Florence*
*Office Services and Related Technology Instructor*
*Correctional Training Facility*

The Teacher's Aide position was a very satisfying assignment and it confirmed a famous quote by Mahatma Gandhi. Gandhi said, "The best way to find yourself is to lose yourself in the service of others." I find truth in this statement because for so many years of my life, it was all about me. When I functioned in a self-centered manner, I was not my "true self." Helping the men in the OSRT vocational program was gratifying and as that experience became more about serving them, I found myself returning to what I now consider, my true self. In the Alternatives to Violence Project, we believe in a concept that we call, "Transforming Power." Transforming Power played a major role in the atmosphere that eventually existed in the OSRT classroom. Initially, the OSRT classroom consisted of approximately 30 African American, Asian, White, and Hispanic prisoners. Many of the men in the class were gang members and others were individuals who only associated with men of their own race. To give you a better understanding of Transforming Power I will share my interpretation of this concept.

There is a power that works through us and between us – a transforming power – that can change a destructive situation into a cooperative one. In AVP, we call it Transforming Power. Transforming Power has always been and will always be the heart and cornerstone of the Alternatives to Violence Project. To be open to this inner and outer power, our purpose/intentions must be morally right. In other words, Transforming Power will not enable us to prosper when we have ill/bad intentions. Every person has an inner wisdom that knows what's right and wants to do what's right. There are laws of harmony in our world of inter-relationships with other people.

Here is one way to understand Transforming Power. At the core of every human being is a jewel, a blazing spark of the Divine. This is the "true core' of every person, the foundation, the center. And when that brilliant core shines in its full glory, it reaches out beyond the person to shed its light on everything around it, to connect with everything and everyone.

Unfortunately, in every human being, that jewel of light is covered by many layers of crud and filth. Our fears, insecurities, pain and our defensive walls cover the jewel and dim its brilliance. Our prejudices and our pride will not let the light shine forth. Our narrow egos tell us that the crud and filth, rather than the jewel, is who we are. So instead of identifying with who we really are, we believe we are the people whom we have become, based on our life experiences.

But it is important to remember that regardless of how many layers of crud and filth cover the jewel, the jewel is constantly shining and can never be diminished. Inside the shell of darkness, it still shines as brightly as ever, and every now and then it blazes through a crack. It blazes forth when we behave in a manner that exemplifies humanity at its very best.

The crud and filth can hide the light momentarily but can never extinguish it.

Transforming Power is that force in the universe which can burn away the crud. And it always begins within. I cannot burn away the crud that hides your jewel. What I can do is allow Transforming Power to do its work in me, to burn away the layers of fear, prejudice and pain that hides my shining core, and let my light shine forth as an invitation for you to do the same.

This is what I experienced as a Teacher's Aide, in the OSRT classroom. As I became more in touch with my true self and let the light from my inner core shine forth, the men in the program did the same. Once the men made note of the fact, I did not bring prison politics into the classroom, and I assisted everyone equally, regardless of their race, they followed my lead. There was harmony and collective cooperation taking place in the classroom, and I attribute that development to the concept of Transforming Power.

By actively participating in self-help groups, I was aware of upcoming future events. The Office of Restorative Justice Ministry was hosting a Victim's Reflection Retreat at CTF on October 21, 2010. I received an invitation to attend this event.

On the day of the retreat, participants met in the institution gymnasium. We assembled into several small groups. There were a couple of people from the ministry in each group. One of the women from the ministry informed us her brothers were gang members and she explained the impact their gang related activities have had upon their family. She also had been visiting a brother, who is serving a life sentence. She informed us the last time she visited him at Pelican Bay, he was in the hole for an assault charge. Therefore, she had a non-contact visit with him. In other words, there was a sheet of glass between her and her brother. She could not touch or hug him, and they could not enjoy the food available in the visiting room.

The woman told us she looked at her brother and told him she had driven twelve (12) hours from Los Angeles to Crescent City to visit him, and this is what she receives in return; a visit with a sheet of glass between them. With tears rolling down her face, she told her brother she cannot continue to support him since he is more dedicated to the gang than he is to his own family. She advised him she would not visit him until he changes his behavior and his priorities.

The woman was crying as she told us this story. That was simply one of the many stories we heard that conveyed the impact our criminal behavior has had upon our families and victims. As I listened to her words, I reflected upon all the people whom I have directly or indirectly victimized, through my ignorance or inconsideration of others. When I contemplate the difference between prisoners who undergo a positive transformation of rehabilitation and those who do not, I believe the former gains a deep understanding of the harm we have caused, while the latter does not. The document below gives a brief description of what took place at this three (3) hour retreat.

*The Office of Restorative Justice Ministry "Families of the Incarcerated" held a Victim's Reflection Retreat at the Correctional Training Facility October 21, 2010. Mr. Hunter is commended for his willingness and courage in volunteering for participation in this extraordinary revealing workshop.*

*The three-hour retreat was conducted by Amalia Molina, Director of this ministry, along with three accompanying members of the ministry; Ms. Brenda Ramirez, Rita Chavez and Louis Cortina. Participants were placed into four groups with one member of the ministry in each group. The requirement was to openly discuss their crimes and the impact their actions had on families and the victims.*

*J. Kramer*
*Staff Sponsor*
*Correctional Training Facility*

In addition to the various workshops, activities and events conducted by self-help groups, we also sponsor campaigns to raise funds for charitable causes. When a self-help group decides to hold a fund-raising drive, we prepare flyers and advertise the cause on the institution's closed-circuit television system.

Once I have informed the general population of the cause, prisoners are at liberty to make donations. Prisoners fill-out what is known as a Trust Withdrawal Form that authorizes personnel in the institution's Trust Office, to deduct the specified funds from his account. The document below briefly describes a donation provided to the Bakersfield Pregnancy Center, on April 4, 2011.

*The Bakersfield Pregnancy Center is a non-profit organization that provides pregnancy exams, material assistance, abstinence education, post miscarriage peer counseling programs, and medical pregnancy verification to expecting mothers in their time of need.*

*The Fathers Behind Bars Inmate Activity Group, here at CTF Soledad, endeavors to assist community programs* *that aide and promote healthy parenting. Through this donation drive we were able to raise approximately $1,000.00 for this worthy cause. Mr. Hunter is commended for his generous donation. This act is indicative of his desire to give back to our surrounding community.*

*K. Heinly, CCI*
*FBBG, Principal Sponsor*
*CTF – Soledad*

Soliciting donations from the general population is one of the methods self-help groups use to make donations to charitable causes. The other method that enables us to make contributions to society is food sales. To sponsor a food sale, we contact vendors such as Costco, Round Table Pizza Hut, Kentucky Fried Chicken, etc. Once we receive the quotes of what we will pay for a certain item, we mark up the price by a small percentage. We then donate a portion of the proceeds to a charitable cause. Following an AVP food sale that we conducted in March, on May 7, 2011, we made a financial contribution to a youth group. It was a decision made by me and the other AVP facilitators.

*On March 7, 2011, the AVP ILTAG (Inmate Leisure Time Activity Group) group of inmate facilitators came to a consensus and donated $500.00 from the AVP trust account to "Continuing the Dream", a youth group conference held in Southern California on April 10, 2011. (See attached letter from Roy Mabry, CTD Chairman). The Alternatives to Violence Project facilitators are commended, as a whole, for realizing the importance of this conference. I would like to take this opportunity to acknowledge the monetary contribution.*

*Inmate Hunter is commended for feeling this was a worthy cause and for his continued commitment to a peaceful community inside and outside of prison.*

*J.A. Soares*
*Associate Warden*
*Central Facility*

On September 14, 2011, I met a very interesting woman who held a GOGI (Getting Out by Going In) seminar in the gymnasium at CTF. Her name is Coach Mara Leigh Taylor. She is the founder of Getting Out by Going In. Coach Taylor created this organization to support her work which began in 2002 with Federal prisoners housed at FCI Terminal Island, in San Pedro, California.

Thousands of inmates working with Coach Taylor over a ten-year period, developed the Positive Decision-Making Tools of GOGI. Coach Taylor and prisoners developed these tools, by combining evidence-based methodology for changing behavior, with suggestions and concepts shared with prisoners. Below is a copy of the document I received for attending the GOGI seminar.

*Mr. T. Hunter attended a two-day seminar sponsored by the Balanced Reentry Activity Group (BRAG). Coach M.L. Taylor presented this seminar, representing Getting Out by Going In (GOGI). GOGI is a 12-tool self-help, self-corrective educational correspondence course. After an introduction, question and answer period, the participants formed small groups (10-15 members) to discuss topics chosen by Coach Taylor. This format included such topics as "how to use one of the GOGI tools to make the participant a better man", "how to best affect the youth in a positive manner utilizing one of the GOGI tools" and "how to make a positive change within the prison system using one of the GOGI tools". Mr. Hunter is commended for his participation in this self-development group.*

*P. Weston*
*Principle Sponsor*
*Balanced Reentry Activity Group*

The actress, Eva Longoria, presented Coach Mara Leigh Taylor with the 2011 California Community Foundation Unsung Hero Award, before an audience of more than 500 attendees at the awards ceremony. Following her extensive work with the women in Los Angeles county jails, Coach Taylor received an appointment, as Educational Development Administrator at Los Angeles County Sheriff's Department.

# CHAPTER 14

## SELF-REFLECTION

After reaching the understanding that resulted from participation in self-help groups and the relationships formed with those I have met along this journey, there came a time in which I had to ask myself a serious question. How did my life take a turn that led to me becoming someone who would kill a friend? Self-refection and analyzing my past has enabled me to understand how and why I have made the mistakes I have made throughout my life.

There was nothing remarkable about my childhood. I was a good kid who never gave my mother any problems during my youth. My mother raised me, and I do not know and have never known my biological father. My mother is a Baptist, so my seven siblings and I attended church on Sundays and certain weekdays. I attended school regularly, always completed my homework, and my grades were probably average. When I consider my efforts in school, I believe I did just enough to get by and never applied myself to my full potential. My siblings and I never fought among ourselves and my mother and stepfather always expected us to be, at our best behavior. We said "yes sir and yes mam" to not only our parents but our elders, as well.

I believe I became conscious of the implications associated with never having a relationship with or knowing my biological father, when I was in grade school. Frequently, on the first day of school the teacher requested each student stand, introduce ourselves to the class, and tell everyone our parent's occupations. As I would listen to my classmates introduce themselves and proudly announce their parent's occupation, I sat nervously wondering what I would say when it was my turn to speak. Though my teachers may have had the best of intentions, I am certain they never considered the possibility that some students resided in single-parent households and may not be proud of their parent's occupation.

I can remember how much it hurt me when I was a kid that my father did not want to be a part of mine or my mother's life. He is responsible for bringing me into this world but did not assume any of his parental responsibilities. The hurt from not knowing my father or what type of person he was, eventually made me angry, bitter and resentful.

As I got older, I convinced myself, through self-talk, not having or knowing my father did not matter. The truth is, I did care, but to cope with these feelings/emotions I suppressed them. I internalized my feelings because I did not know how to express them, and I did not feel comfortable discussing them with anyone. My stepfather came into my life when I was 12 years old. By then I had decided I no longer needed a father, so I rejected him. I did not consider him a replacement for my father, even though he was a good man and an ideal male role model. To my regret, I did not put forth an effort to establish a father-son relationship with him.

Unlike many men in prison, I cannot attribute my violence to behavior that took place in my home. I never witnessed violence in my home, no one in my family used drugs or alcohol and my mother and stepfather taught me the difference between right and wrong. My parents always earned an income in a legal manner and there was structure in our home.

There came a point in time during my incarceration, in which I reached the conclusion, the technicalities involved in my arrest and conviction, do not matter. In many ways, I am appreciative of my years of confinement. A transformation took place during my incarceration that would not have been possible had I remained a member of society. I say this because, prior to my arrest, I was always gainfully employed (worked for a living) and payed my taxes. On the surface, I appeared to be a functioning member of society and it would have been impossible for anyone to convince me I needed to pursue any type of self-improvement. However, eventually, the realization that I had killed a friend, ruined the lives of many and was serving a life sentence, convinced me otherwise. By exploring my past, I was able to see how a young boy with good intentions, became an adult who carried a loaded weapon and eventually, killed a close friend.

As I have stated at several of my parole board hearings, I accept the record as being true and correct. On the night of February 25, 1985, I was/am solely responsible for the senseless, violent and untimely death of my friend, Darryl. My actions deprived Darryl's friends and family of his presence in their lives and prevented him of all that he could have realized and accomplished had I not shortened his life. I also take full responsibility for emotionally traumatizing and victimizing my girlfriend, and my community, by committing this violent act in my girlfriend's presence and within a residential neighborhood.

The crime I committed did not occur because of any significant factors that took place on that fatal night. Instead, the following causative factors contributed to and led to the offense I committed.

- My impulsive behavior
- My distorted self-image
- My unresolved childhood issues
- My possession of a loaded firearm

- My lack of sound morals and values
- My selfish and self-centered thinking
- My detachment from my true emotions
- My reckless and irresponsible lifestyle
- My inability to cope with stressful situations
- My tendency to make poor decisions/choices
- My reliance upon violence to resolve conflicts
- My failure to consider the consequences of my behavior/actions

Meeting Bruce Hodgin during my participation in the Kairos program was truly a blessing from God. I am so appreciative of his offer to correspond with me because it marked the beginning of the transformation that enabled me to become the man I am today. When it became clear to me that Bruce and his family loved and cared about my well-being, I began confiding and sharing my inner-most feelings with them. Sharing my deepest feelings with them proved to be the key factor in establishing meaningful relationships/friendships, with my extended family.

For most of my life, I never revealed anything personal about myself to people whom I considered friends. It was during my period of confinement that I realized I had never been a good friend and I never had a good friend. I came to this conclusion because I now understood the dynamics involved in a real friendship. Furthermore, through my interactions with the Hodgin and Bosco family, I learned the true meaning of unconditional love. It's unfortunate I allowed my feelings of anger, bitterness and resentment to separate me from my biological family when I left home at the age of 15. However, it is fortunate that during my journey, the Hodgin and Bosco families embraced me, and became my extended family. I am convinced the relationships I established with them played a major role in the way I processed and received the information conveyed in self-help groups/programs.

In the past, I believe my image of self was delusional, and out of touch with reality. However, today I believe my perception of self is consistent with how others perceive me. I believe I am a conscious, responsible, and goal oriented, person. As someone who respects, loves, and cares about others and myself, I no longer place others or myself in harm's way. I can establish and maintain healthy, positive and meaningful relationships, and I can honestly say I respect all forms of life. I understand and accept my role in my family, community and mainstream society.

Through the investments that others have made in me, and by confronting my demons and addressing my unresolved issues, I amended many of the character flaws, which led to my incarceration. I corrected my behavior/thinking and rehabilitated myself through the assistance I received from those I have mentioned, and so many others who have assisted me during my period of confinement. The programs mentioned, and all the other programs made available to me by the California Department of Corrections and Rehabilitation helped me confront my self-created deficiencies and become the person I am today.

The skills I acquired from partaking in prison vocational trades, has done wonders for my self-esteem, sense of self-worth and overall self-confidence. As much as I regret my 30 years of incarceration, I realize were it not for my period of confinement, I could not have realized such gains.

I am sincerely sorry for the crimes I committed that violated not only the laws of society, but God's laws as well. I am sorry for the pain and suffering I inflicted upon those whom I have victimized, either directly or indirectly. Though I cannot restore the life I have taken, at a certain point in time I realized I can learn from my mistakes and live my life in a fashion that demonstrates my desire to make amends. I made a conscious decision to become a better person by discarding my flaws and replacing them with what I consider admirable qualities/ characteristics. I do not want people to remember me as someone who murdered a friend, committed other shameful acts, and forfeited all that the better aspects of life entails. Through my day-to-day conduct, I make a conscious effort to do whatever I can to have a positive effect on those around me. I make myself available to my community and certain organizations, to encourage others not to make the mistakes I have made in the past and give back to society.

During my 30 years of incarceration I served time in some of California's most violent prisons. Riots and melees were very common. Fortunately, fellow prisoners never stabbed me, and prison guards never shot me during riots. I never suffered so much as a minor injury. There was a time when I attributed this blessing to my ability to defend myself. However, when I became a more enlightened person and considered the many instances in which I could or should have lost my life, I give all the Glory to God. For many years, I have been totally convinced God watched over and protected me when I was in the "Belly of the Beast".

When I think about my participation in countless self-help programs/groups and the transformation I have undergone, I believe God has a plan for my life that will soon manifest. I appeared before the parole board several times before the board granted me parole. Along the way, the parole board found me suitable for parole 3 times, before the state granted my freedom. Governor Gray Davis rescinded my parole date once, and Governor Jerry Brown rescinded my parole date twice.

In the beginning, I took my denials of parole, personal. However, several years prior to my release, I formed the opinion, the parole board was denying me parole, because the time of my release had not yet arrived. I no longer placed my fate in the hands of the California Board of Parole Hearings,' presiding commissioners. Instead, I placed my fate in the hands of a much Higher Power. I put my faith in God that when He determined it was time for me to return to society, no one could interfere with His plans and the gates would open. ***For only God can open doors that no man can close, and close doors that no man can open***. My release from prison and my second chance at life, are due to the Mercy, Love, and Forgiveness of God. For that I am eternally grateful, and for the remainder of my life I will strive to serve God and be the man that He intended me to be. I am certain my efforts to live up to God's expectations of me, will be a life-long quest, in which I will gladly pursue.

# CHAPTER 15

## THE END OF MY 30 YEAR PRISON JOURNEY

On the day of my release, December 4, 2014, Bruce, his wife Connie, and his brother and sister in-laws, Sebastian and Victoria Bosco, arrived at the Correctional Training Facility, at 7:00 am. Approximately, three hours later, the authorities completed the parole release process, and eight other prisoners and I, boarded a transporting Van. The officer in charge, advised me I had friends in the parking lot who were waiting to take me home. The officer then advised the other prisoners, they were going to the local Greyhound Bus station, that would provide their means of transportation. As we left R & R (Receiving and Release), the officer drove towards an RV (motor home) parked in the parking lot. Suddenly, Bruce, Connie, Sebastian and Victoria immerged from this vehicle. I then realized they had arrived, via Bruce's Motor Home. One of the parolees made the comment," Brother, you are traveling home in style". Another parolee said he has paroled more times than he can remember, and he has never seen anyone parole in an RV. When I entered the RV, I discovered Bruce had brought along his little dog, named Lola. This was the first time I had contact with a dog that was a pet. During my period of confinement, my contact with dogs, involved canines trained and utilized by the Security Unit, to sniff-out drugs and conduct searches. I enjoyed playing with Bruce's dog, Lola, during our trip to Saratoga, California.

Approximately, ten (10) years prior to my release from prison, I wrote a letter addressed to the Vital Records Office, in the state of West Virginia, requesting an official copy of my birth certificate. Once a copy of my birth certificate arrived, I sent it to my dear friend, Bruce. When we arrived at Bruce and Connie's home, in Saratoga, Bruce and I transitioned from the RV to his SUV. He then went into the glove-box to retrieve and hand me, my birth certificate. Several years ago, I had informed Bruce of my plan to go to the Social Security Office and Department of Motor Vehicles, on the very day of my release from prison. Well, that day had arrived.

When Bruce and I arrived at the Social Security Office, I stood in line and waited for my turn to speak with one of the representatives. In a matter of minutes, I approached the woman at an open window. Immediately, I greeted her by saying, good morning and asking her, how she was doing. She replied, good morning and said she was doing well. I then handed her the copy of my birth certificate and requested a new social security card. Shortly thereafter, I was issued a temporary social security card, and informed my official social security card, would arrive in seven (7) days.

Once my affairs at the Social Security Office were complete, Bruce and I drove to the Department of motor vehicles. When we arrived, the clerk issued me a number that indicated there were 30-40 people ahead of me. Instead of standing in line, Bruce and I remained seated, until the clerk directed me to a specific window. When my number came up, I approached the person at the window and informed her I wanted to take the written portion of the DMV test. I produced my birth certif-icate and temporary social security card, for identification purposes. To cover processing fees, I used a portion of the $200.00 (gate money) that I received from the California Department of Corrections, at the time of my release. Then, the cashier directed me to a computer, so I could take the written portion of the DMV exam. Bruce was standing behind me as I took the exam, and he noted I scored 100 %, correctly answering every question.

I explained to Bruce, that prisoners serving determinate sentences, participate in a Pre-Release program that prepares them for their re-entry to society. In this program, one of the benefits is a Department of Motor Vehicles manual that prepares them for the DMV exam. The Pre-Release program excludes the participation of life-term prisoners, such as me. Therefore, we do not qualify for any of the benefits associated with the program, including access to a DMV manual. I told Bruce, one day I approached the person in charge of the Pre-Release program. I informed him I was serving a life-sentence and realize lifers cannot participate in the Pre-Release program. I went on to explain I anticipated my release from prison would occur within a few years, and I would like to be able to study for the DMV written exam. As I suspected would be the case, he gave me a DMV manual. It has been my experience, during my period of confinement, that whenever I was trying to do something positive/productive, quite often staff members were willing to assist me. Even when it involved breaking the rules. Following my completion of the DMV written exam, the clerk scheduled the driving portion of the exam. I successfully completed that exam, two weeks later, and was issued my driver's license.

As Bruce and I drove away from the DMV, on our way back to his home, he turned to me and stated, "I do not believe you are going to have any problems transitioning back into society." I asked him to explain this statement. He then told me it was the opinion of friends and family members, that I would have great difficulties returning to society, after being in prison for thirty (30) years. I told Bruce it was presumptuous for people who never met me and have no idea of how

I utilized my time, during my period of confinement, to draw such a conclusion. Bruce went on to say, as he observed my interactions with people, I encountered at the Social Security Office and Department of Motor Vehicles, he was convinced my transition would be "seamless".

There are certain factors that can increase the likelihood of having a successful parole board hearing. Factors such as proof of residency, offers of employment, and a legitimate support network. For years, I had presented the Board of Parole Hearings, with parole plans that indicated I could reside in Saratoga, California, at either Bruce and Connie Hodgin or Sebastian and Victoria Bosco's home. In addition to these two options, I also had a third option of residing at the Little Orchard Veteran Transitional Housing Program, in San Jose, California. For many years, the Board of Parole Hearings, advised me it was perfectly fine for me to reside with the Hodgins or Boscos, upon my release. However, at my final hearing, they insisted I parole to the Veteran Transitioning Housing program. Of course, I agreed to do so.

I had learned about the Little Orchard Veteran Transitioning Housing program, from a resource guide I acquired during my period of confinement. I wrote a letter to the Director of the program, and she sent me a brochure and other documentation, pertaining to the program. I learned the program consisted of a dorm equipped with three-hundred (300) beds, and ten apartment units. Two veterans share each apartment unit. I informed the Director, I am a life-term prisoner (serving a 17-year to life sentence) and the Board of Parole Hearings will determine the time of my release from prison. I also informed the Director, of my many years of confinement and my belief the Board would release me in the very near future. I requested she place my name on the waiting list for one of the ten (10) apartment units and she agreed to do so.

Whenever I received a parole denial from the Board, I contacted the Director immediately. I would advise her of the denial of parole, and request she keep my name on the waiting list, because my release was just around the corner. Time after time, the Director agreed to keep my name on the waiting list.

Bruce and I went to his home, following our trip to the DMV. We only stayed there briefly and then he drove me to the Parole Office, because I had to report to and meet my Parole Officer. When I checked in with the woman at the front desk, I informed her I am reporting to my PO for the first time since my release from prison. She then requested my name and California Department of Corrections identification number. Moments later, my P.O. came to the lobby, and at that time, I introduced myself and introduced him to my friend Bruce. Bruce, my P.O. and I, then went to his office. Once we were all seated, Bruce informed my P.O. of the long-standing relationship between him and I. In the process, Bruce also mentioned his law enforcement background, as a former San Jose Police Officer. The conversation between the three (3) of us was quite pleasant and interesting. There was nothing confrontational about my P.O.'s demeanor or approach to his initial contact with me. At some point during this meeting, my P.O. advised me of my conditions of parole and presented numerous documents which required my signature. One of those conditions, was my residency at the Little Orchard Veterans Transitional Housing program. The Board of Parole Hearings required I reside there for a minimum of a six (6) month period. I informed my P.O. I would report to the Transitional Housing program later that evening, and my friend Bruce, indicated he would drive me to the location.

As I stated earlier, the Little Orchard Transitional Housing location, is a program for veterans. However, when I arrived at this facility, I learned most of the occupants, were homeless men and women. During certain months of the year, the facility welcomes the homeless. This policy enables the facility to receive additional funding. While I am very sympathetic of those without a home, who are living in the streets, I did not like the atmosphere and what was taking place at the Little Orchard facility. It was not an environment in which one would get the impression, the residents were putting forth an effort to get back on their feet. Though one would expect to find dysfunctional activities taking place at such a location, for me personally, the level of such activities was overwhelming. I did not get any rest that night and I decided to immediately contact my parole officer, the following morning.

The next morning, I called my P.O. and informed him, I did not sign-up for what is taking place at the Little Orchard location. I told him, instead of the facility housing veterans, most of the residents are homeless men and women. I then advised my P.O., that I was concerned about finding myself in a compromising position, due to the type of people living at the shelter. I stated, "We are going to have to discuss other living arrangements because I do not intend to spend another night in this facility." He was all ears, and him and I proceeded to assess the situation. During our conversation, I told him my name has been on the waiting list for one of the ten apartment units at the Little Orchard Transitional Housing program, for a few years. I further indicated that according to the director, my name should come up for an apartment, in about thirty (30) days. I then requested permission to reside with my friends, Bruce and Connie Hodgin, until I was able to move into one of the apartment units, at the Little Orchard shelter. My P.O. granted my granted my request.

Moving into Bruce and Connie's home was great. They reside in an affluent and very quiet neighborhood, in Saratoga, California. The sort of neighborhood in which every lawn is well-manicured, and people are very friendly. It almost did not seem real, that I landed in such an idealistic place. I felt like the biblical character, Joseph, who went from "The Prison to the Palace." Imagine being in an environment, for thirty years, that is so noisy you can barely hear yourself speak. An environment that is uncooperative, violent and downright, uncivilized. An environment in which life has no true value and can end at any moment on any given day. An environment that consists of steel and concrete, and people behind these walls, with hearts that are just as hardened.

For the duration of my incarceration, my bed consisted of a steel slab with a three-inch thick mattress. I now was living in a multi-million-dollar home, in which I had my own bedroom. The bed in my bedroom was about three-feet in height, including the box spring and mattress. This bed had quality linen, fluffy pillows and a very warm comforter. There was a picture window in my bedroom and I remember opening the window, for the very first time, to allow fresh air to enter. In addition to the flow of fresh air, the sounds of birds chirping also found their way into my room. As a guest, I had access to all the amenities within and outside the home. I could go to the refrigerator and cupboards to retrieve whatever I wanted to cook, eat or drink. I had the freedom to use the exercise room or swim in the pool, at my discretion. I truly felt like I was living in a resort.

The week following my release from prison, I obtained an employment position, from Bruce's son, Dan Hodgin. Dan owns a tax consulting firm, in which he provides services to many Silicon Valley businesses/companies. As an employee of Dan Hodgin Tax Consulting, I performed various administrative duties that primarily consisted of, data entry. It was a satisfying feeling to go from slave wages I received in prison, to receiving a legitimate paycheck. Upon receipt of my first check, Bruce accompanied me to Union Bank, where he conducts business, so I could open my first savings and checking accounts. I will always be grateful and appreciative of the fact, Dan Hodgin was the first person to hire me, upon my release from prison.

# CHAPTER 16

## EMPLOYMENT

## JOINING A SILICON VALLEY TOASTMASTERS CLUB

On January 1st, of 2015, I had an interview for an employment position, at Goodwill of Silicon Valley. I was interested in an open Computer Tester position. The position entailed, testing, repairing and refurbishing desktop and laptop computer systems As a Computer Tester, I also would install and run, application and diagnostic software, on these systems. Due to my experience acquired in the Computer Refurbishing Shop, at the Correctional Training Facility, in Soledad, I was confident I was qualified for the position.

Ryan Gleason, the Chief Operating Officer, of Goodwill of Silicon Valley, conducted the interview. On my resume, I had included the last three (3) jobs I held, during my period of confinement. Instead of indicating the name of the prison, I provided the name of my employer and the address of the location. During the interview, Mr. Gleason inquired about my final employment position, as an IEP/ISO Coordinator. He asked me to define the acronyms and describe my actual duties. I told Mr. Gleason, the acronym stands for Inmate Employment Program/

International Organization for Standardization Coordinator. I further explained it was my responsibility to inform prisoners employed by the Prison Industry Authority (PIA) of the various industrial standard certifications available to them. If a prisoner was interested in partaking in the program, I would enroll him in the program, order the testing material and schedule a certification exam. If the prisoner successfully completed the exam, I would order and issue him the actual certificate. Mr. Gleason turned to me and stated, "Oh, so you performed these duties as a consultant for the State?" I immediately stated, "No, I conducted my job as a state prisoner."

It was obvious my reply caught Mr. Gleason, totally off guard. He repeated the words, "You conducted your job as a state prisoner", to which I replied, "Yes." I explained I had killed a close friend, on February 25th, of 1985, and after serving thirty years in prison, the authorities released me, 27 days ago. I went on to explain that at that time in my life, I was a violent person and quite often was in possession of a loaded weapon. I told Mr. Gleason that at the time of my arrest, I suffered from unresolved childhood issues that I carried into manhood. I informed him that after ten years of incarceration I decided to embark upon a journey of self-improvement, to better understand my behavior in the past. Following a brief conversation between Mr. Gleason and I. he expressed his opinion that the man before him evidently is not the man who committed the act of murder, thirty years ago. Mr. Gleason told me he does not have a problem with the crime I committed because my transformation is evident. He hired me on the spot. It was basically, a nine to five job, in which I was off on weekends and holidays.

I enjoyed my computer technician position, with Goodwill of Silicon Valley. The lap top and desktop computers that I refurbished and repaired, were systems donated to Goodwill. In some cases, I encountered systems that were purchased a few years ago. Based on the age of some of the systems I encountered, they had probably been sitting in a garage or tucked away in a closet, for years. Quite often, after troubleshooting a system, I was able to remove a part or parts from one system, or systems, to repair that unit. In many cases, it may have been as simple as repairing a corrupt hard drive, replacing a motherboard, or upgrading the microprocessor chip and system memory. Other cases were more complicated and required more attention and creativity.

Once I repaired these inoperable systems, I installed Windows and additional application software, on each computer. Then, I thoroughly cleaned each unit. The shipping department transported these laptop and desktop systems to Goodwill stores, where they were sold to customers.

The computer repair/refurbishing department at Goodwill, was basically, a two-man operation. My co-worker was a man named, Mike. Mike was very knowledgeable of computers, from both a hardware and software, perspective. As it turned out, Mike has a history with Silicon Valley. He has been in the IT (Information Technology) industry for decades. In addition to previous employment positions with a few of the well-known Silicon Valley establishments, Mike is a former software professor. He is very well-versed, when it comes to programs such as Java and C++. While my employment with Goodwill was a good starting point, after thirty years of incarceration, I decided to pursue an employment position with a well-established and reputable company/corporation. I felt such a company would be beneficial in establishing a noteworthy employment history and be a significant addition to my resume. I concluded, I would go online and apply and submit my resume, to the Home Depot.

On February 11, 2015, Jessica Miller, the HR (Human Resources) representative, for Home Depot, contacted me. Ms. Miller asked me if I was interested in meeting with the store manager, for an interview, on the following day. When I arrived for my appointment, I discovered the man interviewing me, was Mike Hubbard. Following his introduction, Mr. Hubbard asked me a few questions, including my interest in working for the Home Depot. At some point, Mr. Hubbard asked me to explain why I wanted to resign from a full-time position, with holidays and weekends off, at Goodwill, for a part-time position with alternating off days, with the Home Depot. I explained I was aware that all new hires are part-time employees, at the Home Depot. I told Mr. Hubbard I have a strong work ethic, I am a quick study, and I am full-time material. I told him I was confident, I would soon be a full-time employee.

The next thing that happened was like my experience during my interview at Goodwill of Silicon Valley. Mr. Hubbard also inquired about my previous position, as the IEP/ISO Coordinator. Once again, I explained I informed prisoners of the various industry standard certifications available to them, enrolled them in the program, ordered the study material and orchestrated the actual certification examination. As was the case with COO Ryan Gleason, at Goodwill, Mr. Hubbard also believed I conducted my duties as a contractor for the State of California. I immediately stated, "No, I conducted my job as a prisoner, serving time for the state of California." I went on to tell him I killed a close friend in February of 1985, I received a second-degree murder conviction and I served thirty years in prison. I informed him, prison officials released me, sixty-eight days ago. Mr. Hubbard was astonished. He leaned back in his chair, and with a somewhat interesting grin on his face, he said, "I never would have suspected you are someone who has been to prison." He said, my attire, demeanor and articulation, was impressive. Mr. Hubbard made note of the fact, the crime I committed occurred thirty years ago, and therefore, was irrelevant.

Mr. Hubbard, then asked me, would I be interested in working in the Paint Department because an employee in that department had quit the night before. I informed him I did not know anything about paint. He said, that is not a problem...we will train you. When Home

Depot authorities, received the results of my urinalysis, they hired immediately.

For the next twenty-four days, I retained my position with Goodwill. At Home Depot, employees must complete CBT (Computer Based Training) programs, that are directly related to their department. An associate cannot begin working, until he/she completes these programs. In other words, employees are not issued an apron, permitted to work in the store or interact with customers, until we complete our training. To enable my continued employment with Goodwill, the Home Depot scheduled my Computer Based Training period, around my work schedule, at Goodwill.

As I stated earlier, in 2007, with the assistance of several other prisoners, we founded the Toastmasters International Club, known as, "Talk the Line Toastmasters", at the Correctional Training Facility, in Soledad, California. At the time of my release, I had diligently attended Toastmasters meetings, for a seven-year period. As a member of Talk the Line Toastmasters, my activities went beyond simply attending club meetings. As a Toastmaster, I participated in events outside the club setting.

For example, several club members and I, periodically performed presentations in the class rooms in the Education Department. Our intent was to make students enrolled in Adult Basic Education (ABE I &II) and General Education Development (GED) classes, aware of our Toastmasters International Club. We would demonstrate what takes place in a Toastmasters meeting and emphasize the benefit of having effective communication skills. Quite often, the conflicts that prisoners and ex-felons experience both inside and outside the prison environment, stem from the inability to articulate and express one's thoughts and feelings. I would further emphasize, the importance of the ability to articulate and express our thoughts and ideas, during an employment interview. I would inform them that we have a waiting list of individuals interested in joining our club, when an opening becomes available. In addition to our Toastmasters Club, we also sponsored Gavel Clubs, in order that more prisoners could participate. We always received a positive response from our audience, and it was common for several of the students to request to have their names placed on the waiting list.

In addition to speaking to students in the Education Department, I frequently spoke at the Life C.Y.C.L.E (Careless Youths Corrected by Lifers' Experiences) program, at the Correctional Training facility. Several of my friends were members of this self-help program, and they designated me as an honorary member. We functioned as mentors to the younger men who were serving time in the general population, with us lifers (prisoners serving life-terms). So many lifers have missed out on the opportunity of being fathers to their own kids. In many instances, our immaturity, criminal lifestyle and self-centered thinking, is the cause of our 20 to 30 years of incarceration.

The Life C.Y.C.L.E. program presented a chance for many of us to reach out to these young men. It also afforded us the opportunity to acknowledge the pain and suffering we have caused, by our poor decisions, in the past. In this mentoring program we adopted these young men as our own and shared our mistakes in life, with them. We also imparted to them, the knowledge/wisdom we have painstakingly acquired through the years, in hope that they may learn from our shortcomings.

Quite often, staff would request my services, by asking me to speak at important events. For example, a couple weeks prior to my release, a recognition/retirement ceremony for Ms. Jackie Kramer, took place. Ms. Kramer has been Associate Warden J.A. Soares's secretary, for many years. The close working relationship between Jackie Kramer and I, was common knowledge amongst both prisoners and staff. Jackie was the primary sponsor for many of my self-help groups.

As a sponsor, she carried keys that enabled her to open doors that granted us access to the rooms in which we held our meetings and workshops. Jackie also played an instrumental role in the food sale events, conducted by self-help groups. Distributing food order forms to the prison population, marked the beginning of a food sale. After prisoners fill out these forms, I submitted the forms to the Trust Office. Trust Office personnel would then withdraw funds from our personal trust accounts, to cover the cost of the products we ordered. The Trust Office would generate a check to cover the total amount of the food sale, and give this check to Jackie, so that she could deliver the check to Costco or whatever vender we were using at the time.

On a Saturday morning, Jackie would come to the institution, to receive the merchandise we ordered. Self-help group members would unload and transport the merchandise to the Dining Hall, where prisoners picked-up our orders. Without a sponsor, such as Jackie, this process would not be possible. Much of the documentation I received from partaking in self-help activities, contains Jackie's name and signature. Therefore, I was not surprised when staff asked me to be the "key note" speaker, at Jackie's retirement ceremony. At this ceremony, I emphasized the fact, that self-help programs would not exist, without the assistance provided by Jackie and all the other sponsors, at CTF. I let her know how much I had enjoyed working with her over the years, and that her absence will be a great loss, for all concerned.

On February 25, 2015, I decided it was time to attend my first Toastmasters meeting, as a member of society. I went to the internet to search for Toastmasters International Clubs, that were in the vicinity in which I resided, at the time. I was still living in an apartment, at the Little Orchard Transitional Housing program. I located a Silicon Valley Toastmasters Club, known as, "True Talking Toastmasters." Their website indicated the club's contact person was a man named, Matt Lourie. His information included his phone number, so I decided to call him.

When Matt answered the phone, I introduced myself, and inquired as to whether their club, True Talking Toastmasters was meeting that evening. (Their club meetings take place on Wednesdays at 7:00 pm) Matt indicated the meeting will take place, so I informed him I would be there as a guest. At all Toastmasters International Club meetings, non-members are guests. Prior to the commencement of the meeting, guests introduce themselves to the club, tell the members how they discovered their club, and anything else they would like to divulge.

To attend the Toastmasters meeting, I had to ride a VTA (Valley Transportation Authority) bus to a certain point, walk a few blocks and then board a light rail vehicle, at the Curtner Light Rail Station. Once I had disembarked from the light rail vehicle, I had to walk eight blocks, to reach my destination. I arrived at the meeting early. At approximately 20 minutes before 7:00. I had the opportunity to mingle with members and other guests but made certain I did not tell them anything about myself. Shortly after the meeting began, the Sergeant at Arms, made note of the fact, there were a couple guests attending the meeting. When the Sergeant of Arms addressed me, I stood up, introduced myself and informed the membership, I have been a Toastmaster for the past seven years. I went on to mention I had accomplished several Toastmasters Awards, including my Competent Communicator, Advanced Communicator Bronze, Competent Leader, and Competent Leader Bronze Award.

I also informed them I was the first elected President of my club. I then told them what they do not know about my club, is the fact, it is a Toastmasters Club at the Correctional Training Facility, a prison in Soledad, California. I further informed them of my 1985 second-degree murder conviction, and my recent release from prison, after thirty years of confinement. I had decided to be transparent about my past, because if members felt uncomfortable and had concerns about my criminal background, I wanted to know this from the outset. Some people would think it is better to allow people to get to know you and become familiar with you, before you disclose such information. I disagree, because failure to reveal this information from the very beginning, could give the impression I am a deceptive person. To my amazement, after I had finished speaking, every club member gave me a standing ovation.

At the end of the meeting, club members surrounded me and introduced themselves. One woman commended me for having such a positive attitude after undergoing what she was certain, was a very traumatic experience. Several members suggested I join the club. One of the members, a man named Chris Hennessey, a Videographer, offered to pay my club dues. I thanked Chris for the offer, and with a smile on my face, advised him was gainfully employed and capable of paying my own dues. When I expressed my desire to join the club, the club's Vice President Membership, gave me an application. Once I had completed the application, I handed my debit card to the club's Treasurer, to cover both club and Toastmasters International dues. I was now officially a member of True Talking Toastmasters.

My trip home, at the end of the meeting, differed from the one to the meeting. I walked eight blocks to return to the light rail station. Approximately, an hour or so later, the light rail vehicle that would take me back to the Curtner Light Rail Station, arrived. When I arrived at the Curtner station and checked my bus schedule, I discovered it would be an hour and a half before the next bus arrived. Instead of waiting for the next bus, I decided to walk the distance back to the Little Orchard Transitional Housing complex.

I looked forward to attending the next Toastmasters meeting, as a participating member. When I arrived at the meeting, the following week, I had the opportunity to converse with many of my fellow Toastmasters. As it turned out, I was a more experienced Toastmaster and had achieved more awards than most of the club members.

On a regular basis, I volunteered to fulfill functionary roles and delivered a few speeches. It was a totally different experience, to go from attending club meetings in which my fellow Toastmasters were men, to an environment in which the membership was comprised of both men and women.

Three months after joining True Talking Toastmasters, at the first meeting in May, an Executive Body election took place. A member nominated me for the Vice President Education position, and I accepted. Club members unanimously expressed their approval of my nomination, and I became Vice President Education, of a Silicon Valley Toastmasters International Club. Imagine that, an ex-murderer who served 30 years in prison, becoming Vice President Education, of a Silicon Valley Toastmasters International Club.

As Vice President Education, I scheduled members' speeches, verified the completion of projects and served as a resource for questions about education awards, speech contests and the mentor program. I was an important source of Toastmasters knowledge for club members and it was my job to become familiar with all aspects of the Toastmasters education program. The VPE is the second ranking club officer and is responsible for planning, organizing, and directing a club program which meets the educational needs of the individual members. The VPE chairs the education committee. The VPE also serves as one of his/her club's representatives on the area and district councils.

As VPE, you oversee the creation of the club schedule at least three weeks in advance. You ensure the fulfillment of all meeting roles. For example, you wouldn't assign a new member to be the Toastmaster of their first meeting. It was also my responsibility to publish, email or otherwise distribute the meeting schedule regularly so that all members know what's expected and can adjust accordingly if necessary.

I explained the Toastmasters education program to members, and oriented new members to the Toastmasters education program within two meetings of their joining the club. I educated continuing members about the various education awards they can earn, and how they can stay on track to earn them in the least possible time. I arranged meetings to help members complete education awards in a timely fashion. Finally, I verified projects as members completed them and if members qualified, I submitted award applications to World Headquarters. As VPE of my club, I attended Toastmasters Spring and Fall Conference Business meetings and voted on Toastmasters International affairs.

I served a full year, as the Vice President Education. The following year, at the annual Executive Body election, I received a Club President nomination. I accepted the nomination, and club members unanimously approved my nomination. I was now the President of True Talking Toastmasters.

As the person who sets the tone for the club, The President provides helpful, supportive leadership for all the club's activities and is the first official to assume responsibility for the progress and welfare of the club. You motivate, make peace and facilitate as required. Though you must occasionally step in and make a difficult decision, rarely do you do so, without consulting club members and other club officers. You strive to show respect for all members, even when you do not agree with them, and you provide leadership for all.

As club president, I was the chief executive officer of my club and was responsible for fulfilling the mission of the club. I presided at club meetings and the club's executive committee meetings. I appointed all committees and had general supervision of the operation of the club. As president, I was an ex officio member of all committees of my club, except the club nominating committee and I served as one of my club's representatives on the area and district councils. I worked together with all the club's leaders to achieve success in the Distinguished Club Program by encouraging education achievements, building and maintaining membership, attending club officer training and submitting membership dues payments, officer lists and other documents on time. I recognized member achievements by presenting certificates at club meetings, sending personal messages of congratulations and otherwise publicly praising the good work of club members.

During my term as the club's President, I served as the club's representative at the district and international levels. As president, it was my responsibility to provide leadership for the club whenever required. This included creating a nurturing learning environment and enhancing club quality by conducting well-run, energetic, interesting meetings; actively seeking and connecting with club members and officers; listening patiently and offering my assistance; and resolving conflicts as they arose. As President of my club, I also attended Toastmasters Spring and Fall Conference Business meetings and voted on Toastmasters International affairs.

In 2017, I received a nomination for the Toastmasters International Area B6 Director position. I accepted the nomination, and confirmation. As the Area B6 Director, the five Toastmasters International clubs, located in the city of Cupertino, were under my guidance. The clubs under my guidance included Macintalkers Toastmasters, an Apple Toastmasters club, and Amazon Cupertino Toastmasters, an Amazon Toastmasters club.

As Area Director, I was responsible for leading my area by serving the needs of my clubs. To understand my clubs' needs, I contacted club presidents monthly to discuss their performance in the Distinguished Club Program. I also discussed district training and other district events with the area clubs. Furthermore, I followed up on items identified during previous contact with club presidents.

The Area Director is also the area council chair, so I fulfilled my duties, by holding two area council meetings. At area council meetings, I discussed each club's plans and goals in the Distinguished Club

Program and reviewed attendance at club leader training. Regarding club visits, I did the following:

1. Make at least two club visits per club per year:
2. Assess club membership and its leadership's willingness to grow.
3. Determine who fulfills education achievements and the dates of completion.
4. Submit the Area Director's Club Visit Report online.

As Area Director, I participated in Area Director training provided by the district, by attending District Executive Committee Meetings (DECM). The District Director hosts DEC meetings and Area and Division Directors attend these meetings. The District Executive Committee is comprised of Area Directors, Division Directors and the District Director. I submitted reports regularly to the Division Director and District leaders on Area progress. If the number of clubs in the area fell to fewer than four or grew beyond six, I contacted district leaders immediately.

One of my primary responsibilities, was to motivate and assist each club in the area to become Distinguished. As Area Director, it was also my responsibility to coordinate area speech contests. If I chose to do so, I had the option of asking the Division Director for assistance in planning these events.

On November 5, 2016, I attended the Toastmasters District 101 Fall Conference, held at the Biltmore Hotel, in Santa Clara, California. Something miraculous occurred that day, and it is an event in which I will always remember. I stumbled upon three men, whom I originally had met in 2007. All three men are fellow Toastmasters and the relationship between us is rather unique. Please allow me to explain. In 2007, when fellow prisoners and I founded the Toastmasters Talk the Line Club, at the Correctional Training Facility, in Soledad,

California, several Toastmasters members from society, came into the prison to help us establish our club. Arnie Buss, Kristian Crump and Carl Thormeyer, the KSBW weatherman, were three of the men who assisted us. Well, I encountered all three men, at the 2016 Toastmasters Conference. Can you imagine how astonished they were to see me at a Toastmasters Conference? The last time they saw me, I was wearing "prison blues" (a blue prison shirt and a pair of blue prison pants). On this day, I was wearing a blue pin-striped suit. They were even more amazed when they learned I was the President of the Silicon Valley Toastmasters Club, True Talking Toastmasters.

Arnie, Kristian and Carl initially assisted us financially, by helping us pay our club and Toastmasters International dues. They also provided instructions pertaining to how we should conduct club meetings. We received instructions from them, concerning functionary roles, speech evaluations and Executive Body matters. The support we received from these three men was invaluable. It had been a while since they had visited the club at the California Training Facility, so they had no idea the Board of Parole Hearings had granted me parole. I brought them up to speed on everything that had transpired since my release and what was taking place in my life. Of course, all three men were very happy and excited that I had gained my freedom.

Initially, when I decided to become a Toastmaster, in 2007, my objective was to learn the art of public speaking. My sole purpose was to attend meetings regularly and enhance my speaking skills. When I joined this international club, I had no intentions of pursuing leadership roles.

Today, as I reflect upon my Toastmasters experience, I am so grateful I made the transition from simply attending Toastmaster meetings, to someone involved in the leadership of Toastmasters affairs. It has been a very rewarding and enriching experience, to say the very least. In addition to acquiring invaluable leadership credentials, along the way I have had the opportunity to meet and work with some very extraordinary people.

# CHAPTER 17

## CONNECTING WITH THE AVP COUNCIL
## FACILITATING AVP YOUTH WORKSHOPS

Upon my release, I immediately contacted the Santa Cruz/Salinas Valley AVP Council and in a matter of weeks, attended my very first AVP Council meeting. The Council Meeting took place in Marina, California, at Robin and Terrell Keeler's home. Robin and Terrell are AVP Facilitators, whom I have known for about 10 years. Both participated in AVP workshops and activities, at the Correctional Training Facility. We have worked together for many years, and now I was attending a Council meeting at their home. In addition to seeing Robin and Terrell for the first time since my release, I also connected with Linda and Tom McCue, John and Betty Devalcourt, Stacy Hughes, Mimi and Alan Edgar, Vivienne Moore, and several other facilitators that I met on the "inside."

At Council meetings, we discuss upcoming AVP workshops and plan future workshops. We also discuss AVP business matters. Everyone felt the meeting was a very special occasion because I was present and no longer confined. It felt strange being in the presence of my AVP friends, because for the first time, there were no restrictions regarding our inter-actions. For example, on the inside, there were restrictions that prevent-ed us from touching. So, we could not hug and embrace one another. At the end of our meetings and workshops in the prison, they would exit the prison, while I returned to my cell. Linda McCue often would tell me how much should would love to be able to give me a hug, but prison policy does not permit such behavior. Well, tonight everyone at the meeting hugged me when I arrived and when I departed. It is true, that at the end of the night, we all went our separate ways. However, the difference was, at the end of that night, I did not return to a prison cell.

From June 9-11, of 2015, I facilitated my very first Alternatives to Violence Youth workshop. The workshop took place at The Breadbox Recreation Center, in Salinas, California. My Co-facilitators were, Linda McCue and Francis "Pinkie" Weesner. Fernanda E. Ocana, the Community Safety Program Coordinator, for the city of Salinas, was the person who made the necessary arrangements for the kids to attend the workshop. She proved to be a very down-to-earth and pleasant young lady, with an unquestionable dedication to helping at-risk-youth.

To meet the needs of a specific group (such as youth), it is necessary to modify workshops. The fundamental objectives are: to encourage indi-viduals to take responsibility for themselves and the consequences of their behavior; to serve as one another's community; and to find options other than fight or flight when faced with conflict. Which enables participants to deal with potentially violent situations in new and creative ways.

For three days, my team and I conducted an experiential workshop, to develop participants' abilities to resolve conflicts without resorting to manipulation, coercion, or violence. The workshop events place a strong emphasis on the experiences of the participants, building confidence that everyone contributes something of value to violence prevention.

There are other programs used in schools, that rely on certain AVP principles, such as the Help Increase the Peace Program for youth

(HIPP), and a Creative Conflict Resolution to Conflict (CCRC) program that used full-time staff in some California prisons as facilitators. The reasons why transformations occur within these two or three-day periods of time, may include satisfaction of psychological needs for connection with others, discoveries that one can influence a conflict, and a combination of other factors.

Our workshops draw on the shared experience of participants, using interactive exercises, discussions, games and role-plays to examine the ways we respond to situations where injustice, prejudice, frustration and anger can lead to aggressive behavior and violence.

An AVP workshop can help youth in the following ways.

- manage strong feelings such as anger and fear
- deal more effectively with risk and threatening situations
- build good relationships with other people
- communicate constructively in difficult situations
- recognize the conflict management skills you already have
- be true to yourself while respecting other people
- understand why conflict happens
- approach conflict in a more creative and less reactive manner
- consider your own relationship to systems of violence

In this workshop, the primary objective of my team and I, are to establish a safe-haven for these kids, that will enable them to feel safe enough to be themselves. A place safe enough to express their true thoughts and feelings. We inform them we are not teachers and we are not here to provide instructions. We further emphasize our belief that the answers/solutions to whatever difficulties they may be experiencing, are within them.

In this AVP Youth Workshop, the kids were between 13-18 years old. I decided to wait until the second day to share my 30 years of incarceration, with the kids. At a certain point during the second day, I conducted an exercise in which I had everyone stand on the same side of the room. I then asked questions, and if the question applied to anyone in the room, I asked them to stand on the other side of the room. At first, the questions were simple. Questions, such as the following: "How many of you were born in California?", "How many of you like sports?", "How many of you come from a large family?", etc.

Then I began to ask a different line of questioning. I asked them, "How many of you know someone who is in jail or prison?". Just about every kid moved to the other side of the room. I then asked them, "How many of you have a relative who is in jail or prison?" Once again, several of them moved to the other side of the room. I then asked the, "How many of you know someone who was killed?". Once again, several kids moved to the other side of the room.

There is a two-fold purpose for conducting this exercise. First, it will demonstrate to the participants that they have more in common with each other, than they probably would have expected. Quite often kids believe they are alone, when it comes to the things that have happened to them and the circumstances in their lives. During this exercise, they had the opportunity to see, their experiences and circumstances were like the experiences of kids whom they already knew or had just met, in the workshop. The second purpose of this exercise is that it gave me and my co-facilitators an opportunity to determine if these kids have had contact with people who served time in jail or prison. This was important, because the outcome of the exercise, would determine how I would disclose the crime I committed and the number of years I served.

Later that morning, I decided to reveal my crime and period of confinement, during an exercise known as, a "whip." A whip is an exercise in which I will make a statement, and everyone responds, accordingly. For example, in this whip, I made the statement, "Something most people don't know about me is...". I went on to say that, "In

1985 I shot and killed a friend, and I was convicted of second-degree murder and given a 17-years to life prison sentence. I then told them I was in prison for thirty years. I told them I was a violent person when I committed my crime and that AVP workshops, like the one we all are attending, helped me stop my violent behavior. The kids all looked at me, but no one appeared traumatized by the information I conveyed. Instead, each kid revealed something intimate/personal about themselves and the exercise proved to be a success.

As with every other workshop, the atmosphere created by my team and I, made the kids feel safe enough to talk about very personal matters. Information that we were certain they had not shared with many, if not anyone at all. It is a heart-breaking situation when you learn about what some of these kids have been through, at such an early stage in life. It is common for them also to talk about the dysfunctional situation in the home, and their daily experiences. Fortunately, for them, we have resources that we can bring to their attention, that may be beneficial in resolving some of the situations they are facing.

At the end of the workshop, I was pleased with the results I observed. It was obvious the kids were not in the same state of mind they were in, at the beginning of the workshop. I could see the bonds they had formed with each other, and the bonds they formed with the team of facilitators. In the workshop, we do not spend a great deal of time, talking about violence. Instead, we spend most of the time participating in exercises and discussions, that enable participants to acquire communication and social skills. It is my belief that in many cases, violence is the result of the lack of communication and social skills. Since facilitating this AVP Youth workshop, I have facilitated two additional Youth Workshops, in the city of Salinas. In recognition of the work I am doing with youth in the city of Salinas, the mayor and city officials acknowledged me, at a Community Alliance for Safety and Peace (CASP) meeting.

# CHAPTER 18

## ATTENDING THE AVP FALL GATHERING
## MY ROLE AS A PEER REENTRY NAVIGATOR

During my period of confinement, the facilitators who came into the prison, frequently would mention the AVP/California Fall Facilitators Gatherings that they attended each year. It was an opportunity for California AVP facilitators, to meet at a determined picturesque location, to relax, have fun and take care of AVP business matters. The AVP/California 2016 Fall Facilitators Gathering, on October 26-28, took place at Camp Ocean Pines, for three (3) days. The AVP/California 2016 Fall Facilitators Gathering was dedicated to recently released prisoners who participated in AVP, during our incarceration. Instead of referring to us as ex-felons, the AVP community developed another way of defining us. The theme of the 2016 Gathering was entitled, "Celebrating Returning Citizens." The AVP community understands the negative connotations associated with the label, "ex-felon". It was a very kind-hearted gesture, for them to refer to us as "Returning Citizens". I thought it was very creative, and it demonstrated their consideration of us.

To give you a visual image of Camp Ocean Pines, the location of the AVP/California 2016 Fall Facilitators Gathering, I will provide the following information. Camp Ocean Pines was established in 1946 to serve the community as a non-profit camp and a conference center. A jewel on the Central Coast, the camp sits on thirteen donated acres of Monterey Pine forest that nearly meets the ocean shore. Camp Ocean Pines has made memories for more than 100,000 campers – with generations more to come!

They have ten beautifully designed straw bale cabins. They are engineered for passive solar efficiency, and timbers and siding milled from their own wind-felled trees were used to construct them. By staying in these cabins, people experience facilities that use natural resources wisely. Their campus can house 100 guests.

Camp Ocean Pines is a truly unique place for kids to come! Wildlife abounds, with seals and otters swimming by, and deer roaming through the property. The students who come there from urban settings find this a remarkable place! They serve thousands of kids in their summer camps and environmental education programs. They also host students from the Alisa Ann Ruch Burn Foundation and a camp for kids with HIV/AIDS – all who enjoy the benefit of acceptance in this beautiful natural setting.

Adults use the facilities for enriching conferences. Singers, songwriters, sculptors, storytellers, quilters, weavers, flutists, dancers, choirs...they ALL go there. They regularly host weekend and week-long retreats, church groups, marine science focused educational seminars and art focused weekends.

Mere words cannot express how much I enjoyed my time spent at Camp Ocean Pines, during the Gathering. It was such a tranquil setting, and to see deer, otters, raccoons, squirrels and other forms of wild life, after not seeing any form of wildlife for 30 years, was breath-taking. I also enjoyed meeting and working with AVP facilitators, from all around the state.

In December of 2016, my Parole Officer informed me, the Division of Adult Parole Operations (DAPO) had developed a program known as, The Peer Reentry Navigation Network (PRNN). He explained that it is basically a support network for life-term offenders, on parole. It was the opinion of my parole officer and his superiors, that I would be an ideal candidate to facilitate the program. Their opinions were based upon my smooth reentry and transition back to society and the fact, I have not experienced any difficulties. Once I indicated I was interested in facilitating the program, I filled out an application. Once my application was approved, I became a Peer Reentry Navigator (PRN).

The purpose of the Lifer Peer Reentry Navigation Network (Lifer PRNN) is to provide peer-driven support, assistance and guidance, to newly released lifers who are transitioning back to the community, after a lengthily period of incarceration.

The Lifer PRNN was developed in response to the growing numbers of lifers on parole in California, and the recognition that lifers are different from non-lifers in several important ways, such as their:

- Pathways to prison
- Experience of long-term confinement
- Unique reentry challenges

After many months of research and discussion with lifers and stakeholders, DAPO created the Lifer PRNN. Implemented throughout the state, it is designed to be responsive to the specific needs and strengths of formerly incarcerated lifers.

The model consists of three main components:

- Peer Reentry Navigators
- Community Program Partnerships
- Group Networking Meetings

Most lifer parolees have some form of a support system in place, upon their release. In most cases, it is some sort of transitional program and resources available through their parole officer/agent. While these systems attempt to help the parolee transition into society, they both lack something. They tell the lifer what to do without having lived the life of a lifer.

The first component of the Peer Reentry Navigation Network is Peer Reentry Navigators. As a Peer Reentry Navigator, I assist my peers by sharing advice and useful life experiences about navigating the challenges associated with our reentry to society. This advice is more likely to be taken to heart if it is provided by someone who has gone through a similar situation. I have lived and am still living the life of a lifer. I know exactly what help lifer parolees receive, and more importantly, what help we do not receive. I know what challenged me the most and I am now able to make it less challenging for other lifers. As a Peer Reentry Navigator, I have an opportunity to give back and make a difference in another human being's life, which benefits his/her family, community and society at large.

One element crucial to peer support programs is the development of "social capital" for formerly incarcerated individuals. Social capital refers to the quality of social relationships one maintains with family, friends, co-workers, and informal networks. As a Peer Reentry Navigator, I help to facilitate the development of social capital in lifer parolees, by sharing my networks with them and by demonstrating prosocial thinking models and behaviors. Isolation, rejection, and feelings of loneliness have been proven to be factors that contribute to recidivism, for many formerly incarcerated individuals. Therefore, helping them become more prosocial and engaged with their communities, are essential components of the mentoring relationship between me and lifer parolees.

The second component of the Peer Reentry Navigation Network is Community Program Partnerships. The Lifer PRNN collaborates with community-based agencies and organizations that are also providing services to formerly incarcerated lifers. Community Program Partnerships include agencies that offer:

1.  Whole health care
2.  Residential treatment
3.  Employment services
4.  Education
5.  Restorative justice training
6.  Volunteer opportunities

The third and final component of the Peer Reentry Navigation Network is Group Networking Meetings. At the core of the Lifer PRNN are group network meetings. Meetings are open to all lifers on parole and focus on a variety of relevant topics. Group Networking Meetings, are coordinated by the Division of Adult Parole Operations program Parole Agent. As a Peer Reentry Navigator, my role is to not only facilitate, but also to actively participate in these meetings.

These meetings give lifer parolees a forum to discuss any difficulties they may be experiencing and an opportunity, to seek solutions for such problems. Such topics may include:

*   Adapting to technological and cultural changes
*   Navigating systems of care
*   Building social capital and networks
*   Reuniting with family and friends
*   Establishing socioeconomic security

- Continuing to address issues related to life-crimes
- Managing offense and incarceration-related stigma
- Recognizing/modifying prison-based habits and routines
- Identifying opportunities for living amends

On February 16, 2017, I began facilitating Peer Reentry Navigation Network meetings, as a Peer Reentry Navigator. It has proven to be a very rewarding and enriching experience. I look forward to meeting once a month, with my peers, and having the chance to hear what is taking place in their lives. When I consider my participation in the PRNN program, it is really a continuation of my behavior during my final years of incarceration. In addition to participating and completing a host of self-help groups, I also became a facilitator of those groups. Facilitating self-help groups during my incarceration, was an effort to make amends for my wrong-doings, a way of giving back. I am convinced that my effort to make amends for my wrong-doings, will be a life-long undertaking.

# CHAPTER 19

## PUBLIC SPEAKING ENGAGEMENTS
## MY FIRST SPIRITUAL RETREAT EXPERIENCE

My friend, Bruce, is a member of an organization, known as SIR. SIR is an acronym for Sons in Retirement. The members are retired seniors but the founder/founders, decided to refer to themselves as, "Sons".

So, what exactly is SIR? Sons in Retirement is a non-profit, public benefit corporation formed for men. Their mission is to improve the lives of their members through fun activities and events, while making Friends for Life! It has about 150 branches and 20,000 members in Northern and Central California. SIR was founded in San Mateo, California in 1958 and subsequently incorporated as a non-profit public-benefit corporation. The branches cover Northern California from Bakersfield to the Oregon border and Lake Tahoe to the Pacific Ocean.

The organization's purpose is:

> *To provide for the welfare of retired men... who are pursuing*
> *a common goal, the enjoyment of their later years with dignity*

*and pride... through association with other retired men who*
*also have problems that confront men upon their retirement.*

Their member expectations are few. Have the free time, be a friendly, sociable guy, participate in their luncheons and activities and introduce others to SIR so they can join in the fun. Membership is open to men regardless of age, race, color or religion. They are an all-volunteer organization, so their members need to help when called upon. SIR supports no outside causes or interests. They prohibit discussions of politics and religion, soliciting or selling anything to any member.

Most Branches have summer and winter luncheons and a BBQ where wives, partners and guests are invited. Of special interest are Branch activities like golf, bowling, travel, bocce, bridge, poker, walking, hiking, computers, dining out, wine tasting and investing. Their list of activities and events is almost endless, and many are coed. If there is an activity you are passionate about and your selected branch doesn't have it, they will help you start it and involve others.

Each Branch has monthly luncheon meetings where SIRS renew old friendships and establish new ones. Speakers are invited to speak on topical subjects of general interest. My friend Bruce is a member of SIR Branch # 54. He informed his club of my speaking credentials, as a Toastmaster, and I was invited to speak at a luncheon. The luncheon took place on March 8, 2018, at 11;00 am, at the Three Flames restaurant, in San Jose, California.

The title of my presentation was, "My 30 Years with the California Department of Corrections". It is customary for guest speakers to provide background information about themselves, and info concerning their speech, for introductory purposes. However, I informed the SIR contact person that I would not be providing any background information, about myself or my speech. I further explained that if I did so, it would diminish the effectiveness of my presentation.

When I arrived at the restaurant, I was immediately approached by several club members. Everyone assumed I was a former employee of the California Department of Corrections, who had retired after 30 years of service. I was wearing an olive-green suit that is very similar in color, to the uniform worn by correctional officers/sheriffs. Perhaps my attire bolstered their belief I was a former CDC official. One man made the statement, that I should arrest someone who had recently been accused of committing a crime. A member who is a retired attorney, asked me if I was based in Sacramento, during my years with the department. I told him, I was all over the state during my 30-year journey. My statement was true, because I served time at six different prisons, during my years of confinement.

It is not until approximately three minutes into my speech, that I disclose I am a former prisoner. I always enjoy this portion of my speech, because as I scan the audience, the expressions on every face confirm they had no idea I am an ex-felon. At this point, every member of the audience is sitting on the edge of their seat and the room is so quiet, you could hear a pin drop.

At the end of my 30-minute presentation, the entire audience gave me a standing ovation. My speech is always followed by a question and answering (Q&A) session, to give the audience the opportunity to pose any question they may have. Several men in the audience were retired police officers and sheriffs, and they commended me for my success on parole and the accomplishments I achieved along the way. One man was a business owner, and he said he would be willing to hire ex-felons like me but wanted to know how he could determine if an ex-felon was someone who has turned his life around, as I have. I informed him, if he wanted to know what sort of parolee he is dealing with, he can call the individuals parole officer. The parole officer can provide information concerning the parolee's character and other pertinent information.

I received a few questions concerning my transformation and my youth community activities. Many admitted they were naïve, when it comes to the prison system, and my speech had enlightened them on matters in which they were totally unaware. The Big Sir, who reigns over the club like a Chairman, informed me that my presentation marked the very first time that all members gave the speaker, their undivided attention. He said the members are usually engaged in cross-talk or sleeping, during a speech presentation. My presentation was an overall success and I was well-received by everyone in attendance.

When a speaker successfully delivers a presentation at SIR luncheons, the branch shares the speaker's contact information with other SIR branches. Since delivering my initial SIR presentation, I have spoken at two additional SIR luncheons. At the request of SIR Branch # 38, I delivered my presentation at the Villages Country Club, in San Jose, California. Also, at the request of SIR Branch # 62, I delivered my presentation at Mariana's Restaurant, in Santa Clara, California. The response at both luncheons, were identical to the responses I receive at the initial engagement. I am scheduled to speak at several future SIR luncheons.

Earlier, I had mentioned my participation in the self-help group, known as Kairos. In this program a group of Christian men came into San Quentin to spend three (3) days with prisoners. Well, even though prisoners do not spend the entire three days with the men who enter the prison, the three-day program represents a prison version, of a three-day retreat. The Kairos three-day retreat that takes place in society (outside prison walls), is known as Cursillos.

The Cursillos, focuses on showing Christian laypeople how to become effective Christian leaders over the course of a three-day weekend. The weekend includes fifteen talks, called rollos, which are given by priests and by laypeople. The major emphasis of the weekend is to ask participants to take what they have learned back into the world, on what is known as the "fourth day." The method stresses personal spiritual development and is supported by weekly group reunions after the initial weekend.

My dear friend, Bruce, made me aware of two upcoming Cursillos. I decided to attend the Men's Cursillo Spring weekend retreat, that took place on April 5-8, 2018. The retreat took place at St. Clare's Retreat Center, located in the hills of Soquel, California.

St. Clare's has two independent buildings where their retreatants stay in simple, comfortable quarters. The first is St. Agnes Hall and is located to the right of the parking area in line with The Lounge, Chapel and Dining Hall. It has 47 rooms, some of which have private bathrooms and others which share a shower and toilet with an adjacent room, and some of which can host double occupancy. The second is St. Philomena Hall. It has 27 rooms, all of which have private bathrooms and can host either single or double occupancy. Both halls have floors which are at sidewalk level and are particularly appropriate for those with mobility challenges. Both halls have beautiful views of the valley below or the hills above. I stayed in a single occupancy room, with a private bathroom, located in St. Philomena Hall, and the experience was beautiful.

Across a covered breezeway is The Holy Spirit Chapel, which brings the outside in. The pews are comfortable padded wood and the floors are tile. The Altar is made from a giant burl, as are the Ambo and the Presider's chair. Aside from the usual chapel amenities of organ, piano and sound system, the chapel boasts an incredibly beautiful stain glass window behind the Altar. Made from Cathedral-Art Stained Glass, the Holy Spirit window was created from St. Clare's own design by Mr. Hogan, owner of Hogan Cathedral Art Glass Studio in Saratoga, California, a nationally known Cathedral Art Glass studio. It was custom made to fit the octagon shape of the Altar area. The window is inspired by the seven gifts of the Holy Spirit, with flames reigning down from the dove to reignite these gifts in all who attend their retreats

The meeting room is what they call, The Lounge. Registration occurs in the Lounge. It is set up to support almost any type of retreat – either for conferences or meditations. It is equipped with a podium, wireless microphone, projector, large-screen television and other presentation supplies.

Aside from being a meeting space, The Lounge is also St. Clare's living room when it is not being used to host conferences. It is where they hold Registration at the beginning of your retreat and houses the official "Registration Book" (a large, old-fashioned book that holds the history of all who have ever attended a retreat at St. Clare's). It also houses their Catholic Gift Shop, the community bathrooms and their Sacred Heart of Jesus shrine. Because they are in the mountains, their "candles" for the shrine are electric, a unique feature of their Retreat House.

Most of the retreats at St. Clare's end with Holy Mass, the Papal Blessing, and the blessing of sacramentals. While you are welcome to bring your sacramentals from home, you are also most welcome to purchase them at the Gift Shop.

Located in The Lounge, they offer a variety of common – and not-so-common – sacramentals and Christian gifts, including items appropriate for children, meditative readings, Christian movies and music, Rosaries, Crucifixes, medals and scapulars. They also offer a variety of other amenities for those who might forget their soaps, aspirin, digestive aids, or those who simply would like a bit of candy, a soda or a bottle of water to enjoy.

Situated across a covered breezeway from the Holy Spirit Chapel, their dining hall looks out on the beauty of the nature created by God that surrounds St. Clare's Retreat. The hall seats 88 comfortably and up to 100 when necessary. All meals are included in the cost of the retreats.

While it may seem odd to include a deck as an amenity, this deck is enormous and is an engineering marvel. Starting from the Lounge, this enormous cantilevered deck runs past the Holy Spirit Chapel, the Dining Room, an elevated garden and ends at a set of stairs that lead down to the Swimming Pool. All along the deck are lounging chairs and tables where retreatants find a peace filled place to meditate while looking out over the tree-filled valley below.

St. Clare's includes a large al fresco swimming pool that is heated by nature. While the pool is open year-round, it is best in the hot, summer months. It is also a favorite place for our retreatants who wish to meditate by the cool waters and absorb the ample sunshine

For meditating in nature, there are three secluded meditation areas. The first is the Chinese Garden, located at the far end of St. Philomena Hall. Quiet and cool, it invites retreatants to an intimate conversation with God. The second is Madonna Grove, which is accessed near the trail head to the Stations of the Cross. Our Lady, a statue, is enshrined in a cathedral-like grove of Redwood Trees and many hear God's whisper in the gentle breezes at the feet of Our Lady. The third is dedicated to St. Anne and is found on the far end of St. Agnes Hall overlooking the valley below. Located on relatively flat ground, it is a short walk from the bottom floor of St. Agnes Hall and is an inviting place to pray the Rosary.

St. Clare's offers three opportunities to pray the Stations of the Cross. The first is inside the Holy Spirit Chapel with its beautiful meditative space. The second winds its way around the lawn space in front of St. Agnes Hall and is relatively flat. The third invites you to follow Christ up the mountain to Calvary as you hike up the side of a mountain along a switch back trail. Taking over a quarter of a mile and winding through woods and meadows, the Stations end at a life-size cross.

Beyond the cross is Meditation Point with an overlook of the valley below. Each station has its own meditation appropriate for urging you on up the mountain. This is a great hike any time of day but is particularly stunning at sunrise

While some enjoy praying the Stations of the Cross while hiking up the side of the mountain, others may appreciate the less invigorating, but still beautiful Franciscan Way. This walk takes you into a natural high valley with stations that allow you to pray over the life of St. Francis. The walk ends at the Three Crosses, which depict Christ's Crucifixion flanked by the two thieves. Beyond this is a meditation shelter with a bench.

The next and final trail head boasts a relatively flat walk until near its end when it climbs steeply up to Contemplation Rock beyond which is Meditation Point and the life-size Cross that crowns the end of the Stations of the Cross described above. A short way in on this trail there is a path that leads onto yet another trail to St. Therese's Shrine and ends near the beginning of the Franciscan Way. Those who prefer not to walk along the road to the trail head for the Franciscan Way often use this as a short cut.

For three days I felt like I was in paradise. I was overwhelmed by nature's beauty, the sense of peace and tranquility and the sounds of leaves rustling in the wind. It was if I did not have a care in the world. My retreat included nineteen other participants. There was a team of about twenty men, who prepared and served all our meals and provided an abundance of snacks and refreshments, throughout the three-day weekend retreat. Another perk that was included in my weekend experience, was the rule that no one was permitted to bring a cell phone, laptop computer or any other form of electronic device. It should be no surprise, that I did not want to leave St. Clare's Retreat, when the weekend ended.

# CHAPTER 20

## CLUB NEXT STUDENT RECOVERY PROGRAM
## ATTENDING COMMUNITY ACTIVISM EVENTS

My fiancée, Cynthia Yvonne Baugh, is an employee of Home Depot. While at work, on September 13, 2018, she recognized a man whom she had not seen for quite a while. The man's name is Richard Alvarez, and he is a Pastor at Cathedral of Faith, a church in which Cynthia is a former member. During the conversation between Pastor Alvarez and Cynthia, Pastor Alvarez informed her of his Youth Ministry. Cynthia then informed Pastor Alvarez of my involvement with youth and he gave her his business card and requested I contact him. Cynthia called me immediately and informed me of their conversation. Instead of waiting for her to give me his business card, I simply asked her to give me his phone number.

Upon ending my conversation with Cynthia, I called Pastor Alvarez. We spoke for approximately fifteen minutes and I advised him of the Youth Alternatives to Violence workshops, that I facilitate in Salinas, California. I also informed Pastor Alvarez of my incarceration and my involvement with Juvenile Delinquency programs, during my thirty-year period of confinement. Pastor Alvarez indicated he would like to meet with me to discuss his Youth Ministry. He informed me he would be at the Eastridge Mall, in San Jose, California, the following day, for a Community Outreach event. I told him I would be there, and I was looking forward to meeting him.

The following day, I arrived at the Eastridge Mall, to meet with Pastor Alvarez. Since I was not familiar with the mall, I went to the mall's security office and inquired about the location of the Community Outreach event. There were three security guards in the office, and the African American officer, offered to give me an escort. A few minutes later, I was formally introducing myself, to Pastor Alvarez. Him and I engaged in a conversation for more than two hours. It was basically a situation in which we provided each other with background information about ourselves and talked about our personal interests, concerning youth. I became aware of Pastor Alvarez's CLUB NEXT Youth Ministry, that takes place on Sundays, at the Mayfair Community Center, in San Jose, California. He invited me to the workshop that would take place in two days, and I agreed to be there.

On Sunday, September 16, 2018, I arrived at the Mayfair Community Center, very eager to observe Pastor Alvarez's CLUB NEXT, Youth Ministry. Pastor Alvarez is the Director of CLUB NEXT, and him and his wife Sylvia, are the workshop facilitators. As it turned out, CLUB NEXT is an 8-step life skills program. Its design is to help students who are being challenged with life issues like family issues, divorce, absent parents, behavioral issues, anger, addictions, drinking, school absenteeism, and bullying. CLUB NEXT offers a safe place where students can share and discover answers toward a better future. In addition to using my life story to help youth participating in my Alternatives to Violence Youth workshops, I also will be using my story to reach out to youth, in the CLUB NEXT Youth Ministry.

A week or so prior to the event, Pastor Alvarez informed me of the mayor of San Jose's, 9th Annual Crime & Gang Prevention Summit. The event was to take place in the gymnasium at San Jose City College, on Saturday, October 6, 2018. I went to the website and registered to attend the event.

Mayor Licardo and the Mayor's Gang Prevention Task Force sponsors this summit to bring together representatives from the City of San José, non-profit organizations, and local neighborhoods to build and expand partnerships that would help make San José a safer place to live, work and raise a family. The Crime and Gang Prevention summit gives attendees the opportunity to participate in hands-on workshops, engaging discussions and a community resource fair. Workshop topics included the following:

- Gang Awareness 102: An in-depth perspective of gang impacts
- The Dangers and Pitfalls of Social Media from a Youth Perspective
- Gang Awareness 101: Realities of being in a gang, common indicators, and intervention efforts
- Gender Responsive Model: Responding proactively to emerging gang trends involving females
- Gun Safety and Violence Prevention
- Police/ Community Relations: Building community through accountability

Though the registration process required the selection of all 6 workshops, in a preference order from one to six, time restraints restricted our participation to only two workshops. I therefore, attended the Police/ Community Relations and the Gun Safety and Violence Prevention workshops. This was the first time I had participated in a community event and I enjoyed the interaction with attendees and engaging in the brainstorming discussions that took place in both workshops.

On Thursday, October 11, 2018, I will be attending the first Annual California Cities Violence Prevention Network Summit. The event will take place at the Hank Lopez Center, in San Jose, California. This will be an opportunity to learn about current statewide and local violence prevention trends including, law enforcement trends, public health approaches, and justice reforms. Attendees will also participate in three plenaries to discuss key topical issues impacting local violence prevention efforts including; immigration impacts, regional approaches to violence prevention, and juvenile diversion and restorative justice.

Established in 2007, the California Violence Prevention Network brought together 13 California cities to develop a framework for reducing youth and gang violence through comprehensive community-wide action plans. Now 14 cities strong, this member based non-profit organization provides training and technical assistance to communities across the country and internationally in developing balanced violence prevention plans, reducing gun violence, spurring youth engagement, and strengthening police/community relationships.

The California Cities Violence Prevention Network's primary goals are as follows:

- Fostering the development and implementation of comprehensive city-wide violence prevention action plans that blend prevention, intervention, enforcement, and reentry.
- Educating State and federal policy makers about how comprehensive prevention plans can help reduce violent crimes at the local, state and federal level; and
- Serving as California's resource for the development and implementation of comprehensive city-wide plans, with the twin objectives of reducing violence and helping build healthy communities that don't produce violence.

During the latter portion of my period of confinement, I realized the prison environment was my community, since it was the place in which I resided. This new concept played a role in my desire to facilitate workshops, in hope of changing the mindset of those residing in my community. Prior to my arrest, I never considered being a community activist because I did not know anyone involved in community activism. Today, I understand my obligation to do what I can to make my community and society at large, a safer and better place. I am truly looking forward to attending the first Annual California Cities Violence Prevention Network Summit, on Thursday.

For most of my life, I spent a great deal of my time and energy fantasizing about how much better my life would have been, if my biological father had been present. I wanted to believe he would have been an ideal father, an ideal role model, and someone I could have trusted. I wanted to believe my mother's life would have been less complicated, and more enriched, if he had been by her side. At the same time, whenever I made poor decisions in life, or situations were not favorable, I would somehow manage to link those unfavorable conditions, to the father I never had. In time, I came to understand I had developed a victim's mentality, in which I viewed myself as a victim of circumstances that were beyond my control. Using my absent father, as a crutch, to justify my shortcomings.

As a young boy, I can remember throwing myself a pity party, from time to time, indulging in self-pity. Jealous of my childhood friends, who had fathers and jealous of the relationships they shared with their fathers. Often wondering what was wrong with me, and trying to understand, why the man that had brought me into this world, had abandoned me. One day I had a revelation that enabled me to no longer take responsibility for my biological father's failure, to uphold and fulfill his parental obligations. I attribute his absence in my life, as a character flaw, that has nothing to do with me.

In addition to reaching the understanding that I am not responsible for my biological father's absence, I also came to realize something else. I examined my presumption that my father is a great person with many exceptional qualities. An ideal father, ideal husband and an ideal role model. Today, I see this viewpoint of him, as nothing more than the wishful thinking of a young boy. The idealistic image of my biological father, that I conjured up as a child, is highly unlikely. I painted a perfect picture of him, in my mind, and hung on to this belief. Never once considering the possibility, that he may not be such a person. It is possible that my mother and I would have been in a worse position, had my biological father been the head of our household. He could have been abusive towards my mother and I, and anything other than an ideal role model.

My biological father could have been a dope fiend or an alcoholic, and an overall irresponsible individual. The truth of the matter is, it is impossible for me to know whether my life would have been better or worse, if my biological father had been present.

I would like to take this opportunity to make something perfectly clear. It is not my position, and I am not saying that every boy who grows up without his father's presence in their life, will murder someone or make the poor decisions I have made. I can only give account of how I responded to my situation, and how my father's absence, impacted my life.

As a kid, I was unaware of successful men that were solely raised by their mothers, who made significant accomplishments in life. Though I would suspect, in many cases, an older brother, uncle, neighbor or perhaps a teacher, took an interest in them. Somewhere along the way, someone inspired and supported these young boys.

I am referring to the guidance and sound advice that a person receives from a mentor. A mentor is a person or friend who guides a less experienced person by building trust and modeling positive behaviors. An effective mentor's role is to be dependable, engaged, authentic, and tuned into the needs of the mentee. A mentor may share their knowledge, advice, resources, and information about his or her own choices in life. A mentor may also provide motivation, emotional support, and good role modeling practices.

It's unfortunate that no one took such an interest in me, when I was a young boy. I am certain having a mentor would have enabled me to make better choices and use better judgement, in decision making situations. During my incarceration, I took advantage of every opportunity to give positive advice to young men serving time and young boys who entered San Quentin State Prison, to participate in our program for juvenile delinquents. Today, I am pleased I can be a mentor to kids, by sharing my life experiences with them. However, my desires go beyond simply using my life story to help kids. I also have a passion to help men serving time in prison. Please allow me to explain.

At a recent speaking engagement, during the questioning and answering session of my presentation, a woman in the audience asked me where I would like to be in the next five years. I replied, "In five years, my plan is to go back inside California State Prisons, to help the men I left behind." I told her, I was effective when I facilitated self-help groups during my period of confinement, and I believe I would be more effective, as a former prisoner, who has had nothing but positive and successful experiences, since my release. The woman then stated, "I would think inside a prison is the last place you would want to go, after serving a thirty-year sentence." I then replied, "That is because you believe my incarceration was a negative experience, whereas I do not." I went on to explain, were it not for my incarceration, I would not be the man I am today.

My motivation for wanting to go back inside California prisons, emanates from my belief that a prisoner must be free, prior to his/her release from prison. That is the key to returning to society with the correct attitude and mindset. I was free, many years prior to my release from prison.

The truth of the matter is, I was in prison when I was a member of society. I was in prison from a mental and psychological perspective. Prior to my incarceration, I was an emotionally immature person. Very trivial matters would cause me to become angry and out of control. I was totally unaware of my dysfunctional behavior and the source of my anger.

By the grace of God, my participation in prison self-help programs, revealed the connection between my internal anger and my feelings regarding my biological father. For most of my life, I suppressed and ignored my emotions, regarding how I felt about not knowing my biological father. Understanding the source of my anger, enabled me to explore and resolve the emotions attached to the anger. This is truly a case in which the truth, set me free. This explains why so many prisoners suffer the incarceration experience, repeatedly. They fail to get to the root of the problem, concerning their criminal thinking, attitude and behavior.

As someone who was on the inside looking out, the high recidivism rate and revolving door of California prisons, are no mystery to me. It was very easy for me to determine the men who after paroling, would once again find themselves in handcuffs, in the county jail and back in prison. At the same time, I also could deduce that certain parolees would never repeat the incarceration process. The process of reaching such determinations is simple. A person's experience on parole, will be determined by what they are doing and not doing, during their period of confinement. If a prisoner fails to reach an understanding of the root causes of the behavior that lead to their incarceration, that behavior will continue, whether they are in prison or society. The "Reentry" process begins in prison, long before the prisoner's release. However, the correctional system operates in a way that demonstrates the belief, the "Reentry" process begins upon the prisoner's release from prison. If permitted to reenter the prison system, I am certain I could effectively introduce prisoners to the concept, the reentry process begins prior to their return to society.

# CHAPTER 21

## COMING FULL CIRCLE

After killing a close friend, and receiving a 17 years to life prison sentence, I thought my world had ended. Although I initially blamed others and circumstances, I finally accepted the fact, it was my tendency to make poor decisions that led to my friend's death and finding myself in a prison cell.

There was a time when I would question my attitude, thinking and behavior, in the past. Often wondering why, I had behaved in such a manner. Though I still am ashamed of the behavior that has caused much pain, suffering and the loss of a life, I no longer question or try to rationalize my motives. Furthermore, I have forgiven myself for every act that violated God's Laws or the laws that govern our society. I now am convinced my behavior at any given point in time, in my life, reflected who I was at that time. My conduct at any given time in my life, was based upon the values, morals (or lack thereof), knowledge, information, perception and understanding, I possessed at that time.

This is a concept that I believe eludes most people. Consider how often you will hear people comment on the behavior of youth. Making statements as if the kid behaves the way they behave, by choice. When in fact, the kid is not aware that he/she has alternative ways of behaving or coping with any given situation. There's only a choice in how a person responds to situations/circumstances, when they are aware of that choice. If that kid could do better, he/she would do better. It is like expecting a person who does not even have a GED, to have the knowledge and reasoning of someone with a PhD. One final analogy would be expecting someone with low self-esteem, to conduct themselves in the same manner as a person with a high sense of self-esteem. It has much to do with self-identity, which is the recognition of one's potential and qualities as an individual.

When I think about my own self-identity, when I was a young boy, it explains many of the choices I have made in life. My image of myself was based on the fact, I was an illegitimate child because I was born out of wedlock. In addition to this stigma, I can recall television presentations in which politicians such as George Wallace and Strom Thurmond, referred to my people, as niggers. Not to mention watching footage of events in Mississippi and Alabama, that depicted police beating African Americans as if we were subhuman, and observing men, women and children being attacked and bitten by dogs. Instead of being born into a financially stable household, I am the product of the very opposite. As a kid, I was not aware of scholarships and grants, so I did not believe attending college was a possibility for me. In all honesty, as a kid, I did not believe the future held great things for me. I was truly a person with no "hope".

It is amazing that I did not come to fully understand my true self, until after many years of incarceration. I guess you can say I had an awakening. I came into an understanding I had allowed factors that had nothing to do with me, to define me. For example, I allowed the racial discriminatory behavior and practices of this country, to influence how I felt about myself. In school, I was introduced to history concerning the Founding Fathers and every great or admirable accomplishment achieved by people of European descent.

While learning absolutely nothing about the history, culture and achievements of people of African descent. During my period of confinement, I would address the issues that shaped and formed my self-identity.

Regarding my low self-esteem, for being a member of a race that so often is associated with slavery, I overcame this stigma. I believe it was the intention of the powers that be, to convince African Americans our history began with slavery. Instead of understanding we are descendants of Kings and Queens, we would mistakenly believe we are descendants of slaves. Totally unaware of the rich history of our people that existed, long before our ancestors were subjected to the treacherous Middle Passage journey. African empires existed long before Africans had contact with Europeans. Victorian missionaries liked to think they were bringing the beacon of "civilization" to the "savages" of Africa, but the truth is that Africans were developing commercial empires and complex urban societies, prior to our contact with Europeans. Many of these civilizations were small and short-lived, but others were truly great, with influence that reached far beyond Africa and into Asia and Europe. Today, I am proud to be a descendant of a continent that is so rich in history, diversity and traditions.

Next, was my obsession about not knowing my biological father. If I had remained in the church, instead of abandoning the faith I practiced up until the age of fifteen, I would have come into the understanding I am a child of God. I would have realized, a relationship with my Heavenly Father and knowing Him, is far greater and more important than any relationship that could possibly exist between me and my biological father. For God is the Father of the fatherless. Our earthly fathers are an important source of our genetic makeup, but God is the ultimate source of our lives. He knew us before we were conceived and formed us in the womb. God is the source of our existence, He provides for us, He corrects us, and He loves us unconditionally. Since coming into the understanding, I have a Heavenly Father that guides, protects and loves me, I have been able to move forward in life.

Despite the countless assaults and racial riots/melees that occurred during my thirty years of incarceration, I never suffered so much as a scratch. In the early period of my incarceration, I believed I managed to stay out of harm's way because I was 6" 3, I weighed 250 pounds and I was capable of defending myself. However, one day it occurred to me that staying out of harm's way had nothing to do with my ability to take care of myself. Furthermore, I reached the understanding that the idea that I was taking care of myself, was delusional. All my life, since leaving home at the age of fifteen, I have been under the impression, I was taking care of myself. Today, I realize God has had his hand on me and has been taking care of me, long before the day I left home.

From the beginning, God knew my steps and the mistakes I would make in life. I do not believe in coincidences and I believe everything happens for a reason. When I arrived at Folsom State Prison, I can remember thinking my life was over and I am going to accept the hand I have been dealt. The attitude I had at that point in time, took my violent nature to the next level because I was in a very violent prison and serving a life sentence, which meant I may possibly die in prison. If I was going to spend the rest of my life in prison, never returning to society or being in the presence of my family, what did I have to live for.

One thing I know for certain is that a man without hope, fears no man, fears no situation, and does not fear death. Years later I would realize my incarceration did not mark the end of my life, but instead, would be the beginning of a purpose driven life.

When I decided to participate in self-help groups, I simply intended to attend the meetings for eight weeks or whatever the duration of the program may have been. My objective was to gain the knowledge offered by the program, and that was the extent of my expectation. However, I discovered after completing many of these programs, I developed a sense of obligation to pass on what I had learned, to fellow prisoners. Surprisingly, my peers were very receptive of my efforts to encourage them to challenge many of their beliefs and viewpoints. Though I was volunteering and not receiving any form of compensation for my time, helping fellow prisoners was a very rewarding experience. It was gratifying to see so many of them get loose and free of the forces that were binding them spiritually and psychologically. The same was true of my participation in the Juvenile Delinquency programs that enabled me to connect with youth who were involved in criminal behavior. It was great having the chance to use my life story, as an example of their eventual fate, if they continued to make poor decisions. Suddenly, my life had purpose and meaning.

I am convinced it is my calling to use my life and incarceration experiences, to help make certain the youth of today, do not become the prisoners of tomorrow. I believe many of the issues that caused me to make poor decisions, are the very same issues tormenting today's youth. It is my opinion that one of the greatest problems in our country, is absent and noninvolved fathers. There's the situation in which the father is absent from the home, and the situation in which the father is in the home, but not involved in his child or children's lives.

No one would ever deny the importance of a mother's role when it comes to raising a child. A good mother has been historically expected to contribute her whole life to her family. Mothers have been the glue that holds a family together because it is up to them to provide the loving care and support needed by growing children. The nurturing a mother provides is unparalleled and a vital part of a child's care.

However, there are studies that focus on the importance of gender-specific parents for child rearing. The presumption that children need both a mother and a father is widespread. The research on fathering is indisputable: Fathers have a crucial role to play in the cognitive, social, and emotional development of their children. An involved father is one who is engaged, available, and responsible. He is sensitive and supportive, nurturing and affectionate, and comforting and accepting. Having such contributions from both parents, increases a child's chances of developing into a balanced, and well-rounded person.

When I was a kid, I was very disturbed about my father's absence, and yet I never shared those emotions with anyone. I never voiced how I felt about his absence, and I never expressed those feelings in writing. No one ever asked me about my emotions, concerning my absent father. So, those emotions remained bottled up inside me, for most of my life. I was basically a walking time bomb, that could explode at any moment.

I would suspect that in many cases in which young boys are behaving badly, the father is absent or noninvolved in his son's life. In my encounters with many juvenile delinquent boys, both inside and outside of prison, this has been the case. In such instances, I have found I was the only person who ever asked about their feelings, concerning their absent or noninvolved fathers. Just like me, these young boys are walking time bombs, that could explode at any moment.

One of my main concerns, is how often juvenile delinquent boys do not receive any form of help, until after they have entered the criminal justice system. It is my plight to reach these boys before they explode and destroy lives, including their own. I believe we can do so much more to reach out to youth, when it comes to intervention and prevention. It is unfortunate, that I was not able to resolve the issues that were preventing me from being my true self, until after my incarceration. In the process I have gained a better understanding of myself, other people and the dynamics involved in establishing and maintaining meaningful, positive and healthy relationships. It is not necessary that any child's life takes the same course that mine has taken, for him/her to turn their life around.

I believe God has spared my life and given me a second chance because He has a plan for my life. I believe this plan has manifested in my current efforts to mentor and help at risk youth. I also believe God's plan includes my role as a Peer Reentry Navigator, for life-term offenders, on parole. However, I believe the work I am currently doing to help youth and life term offenders on parole, merely represents a very small fraction of the work I will be doing in the future, to reduce the violence taking place in our society. I am a non-violence advocate, and for the rest of my life I will do whatever I can to convince kids and adults, violence is never the solution. It is my way of trying to make amends for the damage and destruction, my poor behavior has caused.

30161430R00131

Made in the USA
San Bernardino, CA
22 March 2019